WITCHES

WITCHES

UNA WOODRUFF

Written by

COLIN WILSON

CRESCENT BOOKS

New York

This 1988 edition published by Crescent Books, distributed
by Crown Publishers, Inc., 225 Park Avenue South,
New York, New York 10003.

Designed by Steve Henderson

Printed in Singapore

Library of Congress Cataloging-in-Publication Data
Woodruff, Una.
Witches.
Includes index.
1. Witchcraft—History.   I. Wilson, Colin, 1931– .
II. Title.
BF1566.W78   1987   133.4′3′09   87–20191
ISBN 0-517-65494-6 (Crown)

h g f e d c b a

CONTENTS

INTRODUCTION

The most unexpected bestseller of 1926 was a book called *The History of Witchcraft and Demonology* by the Revd. Montague Summers. Issued by Routledge and Kegan Paul as part of their *History of Civilisation*, it was an obviously serious work, full of Latin quotations, lengthy footnotes, and a comprehensive bibliography. What startled the reviewers was that the author clearly believed every word he wrote about the 'enormous wickedness' of witches, warlocks and devil worshippers. H. G. Wells was so incensed by the book that he launched a vituperative attack on it in the *Sunday Express*. *The Times*, equally disapproving, contented itself with the comment that 'the more Mr Summers gives proof of general ability, of scholarship and of wide reading, the more the suspicion deepens that a mystification is in progress and that he is amusing himself at our expense'.

Was it a legpull? Or a cynical attempt to achieve a *succès de scandale?* Apparently neither. The Reverend Montague Summers was a respectable Catholic scholar, editor of several Restoration dramatists, and founder of a theatrical society called the Phoenix, which revived Restoration plays on the London stage. It is true that his name was not to be found in the clergy lists of either the Roman Catholic Church or the Church of England; but this was not — as rumour had it — because he was an unfrocked priest; in fact he had been ordained a Deacon of the Church of England in 1908, a year before he became a Roman Catholic convert. It is also true that he allowed people to suppose that he was a Roman

Catholic priest, and used to say Mass in his own private oratory, in spite of the fact that he had been rejected as a Candidate for the priesthood by his superiors. The gusto with which he recounts sexual details of the satanic rites — even though most of them are decently clothed in Latin may suggest why his superiors had found him unsuitable. In spite of these foibles, Summers was a genuine scholar. And the views he expressed were the views held by the Roman Catholic Church in his own day — as they still are.

These views were what enraged Wells. He simply found it incomprehensible that any sane person could swallow these preposterous superstitions. He could understand how an intelligent Catholic could believe in the existence of powers of evil; but the notion that human beings might have intercourse with these diabolic forces struck him as sheer intellectual perversity. Understandably he thought that Summers must be either a charlatan or an idiot.

He was neither. The truth is that Wells and Summers were simply on different wavelengths. Wells was in love with the vision of science, and with the notion that science will one day uncover all the secrets of the universe. Like his mentor T. H. Huxley, Wells was a convinced Darwinian; which meant that he regarded with pitying contempt anyone who believed that life could exist apart from matter. Like the majority of modern biologists, Wells believed that life is a chemical reaction that takes place in matter, and that a dead body is simply a body in which this reaction has ceased. Since human beings are the highest form of life on this planet — and probably in the solar system — it follows that there are no spirits or demons — and no angels either.

If we reject this view of the nature of life, the position of Montague Summers begins to look altogether less absurd. If life somehow exists apart from matter, then presumably it is somehow capable of controlling matter. That sounds obvious enough, until we remember that a genuine material-ist — or behaviourist — believes that everything we do is as mechanical as water flowing downhill. I am not really writing these words because I want to, but because complex inner forces leave me no alternative; you are not reading them out of 'choice', any more than you are breathing out of choice; these words happen to be the intellectual equivalent of air ... But the moment I believe I can do something because I *want* to, I am assuming that there is some principle inside me that controls this body just as I control a car when I am driving.

But a man who taught himself to drive — as we all have to teach ourselves to live — might well be ignorant of some of the basic principles of the car. He might believe, for example, that it only has one gear, and that it can only travel at ten miles an hour. Where the body is concerned, I am inclined to believe it has a number of 'gears' that most of us do not even suspect. For example, I became acquainted a few

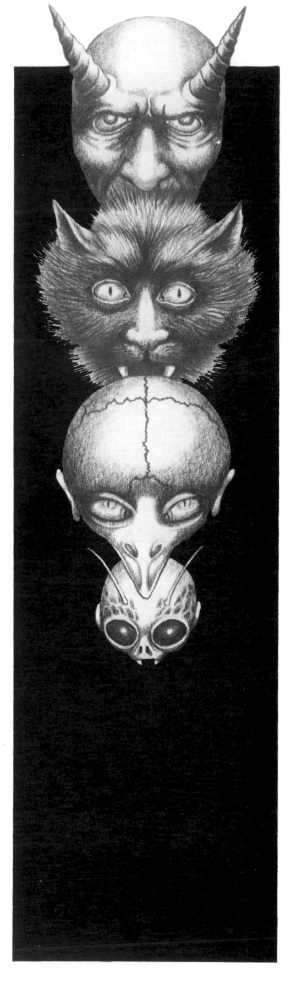

years ago with a young man named Uri Geller, and became convinced that he could read my mind, and also could bend metal by merely rubbing it gently with his finger. I am fully aware of the possibility that he may be merely a conjuror; like the Amazing Randi — trying to duplicate his 'tricks', I end by feeling that he probably does have some 'supernormal' powers I do not understand. He tells me that I probably possess these powers myself, and I am willing to believe him; but I do not seem to be able to engage the right gear.

Again, in a book called *The Occult,* I have described my visit to a 'wart charmer', Fred Martin, who lives on Bodmin Moor. Not only is he able to make warts disappear within a short period — say ten days — but he can also stop bleeding and cure snakebite. He is a 'white witch' who does not know how his powers operate; in fact, he does not believe he has any powers. He tells me that the 'charm' was passed on to him by two old ladies in the 1930s, and that it is a text from the Bible. It seems possible that the disappearance of the warts is 'psychosomatic' — that is, that his belief that the warts will vanish is communicated to the unconscious mind of the person with warts, which then erases them.

While writing *The Occult*, I became convinced that 'psychic powers' are far commoner than we realise: for example, 'second sight' — the power to know what is going on somewhere else — and the power of prediction.

Powers of prediction are probably far more commonplace than we realise. A musician friend, Mark Bredin, who was returning home late one night by taxi when he suddenly *knew* that a taxi would shoot across the next traffic light and hit them. He was tempted to tell the driver, but felt it would 'look silly'. And at the next traffic light, a taxi tried to rush across on the yellow light, and rammed their own taxi...

In this case, it seems clear that the reason for the flash of prediction was that he was tired — after playing in a concert — and his concious mind was utterly relaxed. His unconscious mind somehow sensed what would happen, and managed to communicate it to his conscious self.

Since writing *The Occult*, I have become aware of the work of Sperry and Ornstein on 'split brain research', which seems to me to offer even more plausible hypotheses about the working of the 'sixth sense' or 'paranormal powers'. What their researches have revealed is basically that we all have *two different people* living in the left and right hand sides of the brain — more specifically, the cerebral hemispheres. The person you call 'you' lives in the left — the half that deals with language and logic. The person who lives in the right — which deals with intuitions and meanings — seems to be, relatively speaking, a stranger. If the bridge of nerve fibre joining the two halves is cut — as it is sometimes to cure epilepsy — the 'split' now becomes very obvious. One split-brain patient tried to embrace his wife with his right arm, while his left hand pushed her away. Another tried to button up his flies with his right hand, while the left unbuttoned them. (The left side of the body is connected to the right side of the brain, and vice versa.) A split-brain patient who is shown a square with his left brain, and a circle with his right, and asked to draw what he has just seen, will draw a square with his right hand, a circle with his left.

We are *all* split-brain patients, to some extent; communication between the two hemispheres is poor. I am a writer by profession, which means that my right brain is now sending up the *meanings* I am trying to explain, while the left brain — the 'me' — turns them into words. But I am saying something I have written about many times before, so the process is partly mechanical. If I wanted to capture really deep intuitions about how my mind works, I might struggle for days, and still only express them in clumsy fragments.

Why is communication between the two hemispheres so poor, when there is an enormous bridge of nerve fibres joining them? The reason, I suspect, is that better communication would be, at this stage in our evolution, no advantage. In *The Occult* I discussed the case of Peter Hurkos, a Dutch house painter who fell off a ladder and fractured his skull. When he woke up in hospital, he found he could read other people's minds, and 'knew' all kinds of things about them. He could also 'psychometrise' objects — read their history — by holding them in his hand. The trouble was that this new 'psychic' faculty prevented him from being able to take a normal job of work; he was simply unable to concentrate. Hurkos has since become a famous clairvoyant, and has been able to make a living through the use of his new faculty; but his case illustrates why psychic powers are often a nuisance. There is interesting evidence that many animals possess such powers — perhaps most of them — which suggests that man himself once possessed them. It seems that he has *deliberately got rid of them* because they are not particularly useful to a creature who has to spend his life concentrating upon minute and rather boring particulars — catching trains, adding up figures, shopping in supermarkets (all left-brain activities). Uri Geller told me that he had a severe electric shock from his mother's sewing machine when he was about three — it knocked him unconscious. Matthew Manning, another well-known psychic, told me that his mother suffered an electric shock when she was carrying him. Other psychics have had severe illness in childhood, or been deeply unhappy — all of which suggests that psychic faculties are an accidental by-product of physical or psychological damage — a kind of short circuit. Felicia Parise, a New Yorker who discovered that she could move small objects by concentrating on them — an ability known as psychokinesis — has described how her efforts were unsuccessful until she received a severe emotional shock — news of the death of her grandmother; then a plastic bottle she reached out for moved away from her hand; after the

funeral she tried again, and found she now had the 'knack' of moving things with her mind. And — like the episode of the taxicab, described on a previous page — this also provides strong corroborative evidence that it is that 'other person' in the right brain who is responsible for 'psychic powers'. It was her conscious ego — the left brain — that tried and failed; but a sense of crisis aroused the hidden powers of the right....

H. G. Wells would no doubt have found a dozen reasons for dismissing all this as hopelessly unscientific; and I personally am inclined to sympathise with such an attitude. The world *would* somehow be a more comfortable place if everything could be tested in the laboratory. But after fifteen years of reading and writing about the paranormal, I personally have no doubt whatever that many weird and preposterous phenomena really occur. Poltergeists *do* exist. People *do* accurately foresee the future. Some houses *are* haunted. And a great many people possess a 'sixth sense' that can provide them with information not available to the other five.

And what about witchcraft, the ability to *cause* paranormal events? In a sense, Uri Geller and Felicia Parise are 'witches' (the word applies equally to male and female). But this not what is generally meant by the word. Fred Martin *is* a 'witch' because although he does not regard himself as being in any way psychic or unusual, he does make use of a 'charm' to cure warts. *This* is the kind of power that seems to outrage common sense, even if we can accept the possibility of such oddities as telepathy, dowsing and 'second sight'.

Even in the days before I had started to take an interest in the paranormal, I had met a number of people who were convinced of the reality of African witchcraft. The travel writer Negley Farson told me how he had seen a witch-doctor conjure rain out of a clear sky. Another friend, Martin Delany, told me a similar story of a witch doctor who predicted that heavy rains would cease for precisely two hours for a garden party; the rain — which had continued for many weeks — stopped over a fairly small area for the precise period of the garden party. It seems clear that witchcraft is still a living force in Africa and that it has been witnessed by many balanced and level-headed western observers. In a book called *Ju-ju in My Life,* James H. Neal, former Chief Investigations Officer for the Government of Ghana, tells some baffling stories. His first acquaintance with African witchcraft occurred when he visited a port being built at Tema and was told that a certain small tree had defied all efforts to move it. The most powerful bulldozers failed to tear it out of the ground. The African foreman explained that the tree was a Fetich — that it was inhabited by a spirit, and that the only way to move it was to ask the spirit to leave it for another tree. Finally, the Fetich Priest was called; he asked for three sheep, three bottles of gin, and a hundred pounds if

he succeeded in moving the tree. The blood of the sheep was sprinkled round the base of the tree, then the gin; then the priest went into a semi-trance, and begged the spirit of the tree to vacate it for a better tree, on the grounds that the port would afford employment for many blacks. After various rituals, the priest announced that the spirit had agreed to leave. To Neal's astonishment, a small team of men then had no difficulty in pulling the tree out of the ground with a rope...

This story is interesting because it makes clear the place of 'spirits' — often nature spirits — in witchcraft. This aspect, I am inclined to believe, is more important than anyone has given it credit for. It emerges again clearly in an episode in Laurens Van Der Post's book *The Lost World of the Kalahari*, in which he describes how a guide offered to take him to a mysterious region called the Slippery Hills — the one condition being that there must be no killing of animals. Van Der Post forgot to tell the advance party, who shot a warthog; from then on, everything went wrong. The camera and tape recorder jammed continually, although they had given no trouble before, and the camera swivel failed. They were attacked by bees. Their guide warned them that the spirits were angry; when he tried to pray, some invisible force pulled him over backwards. Finally, he threaded a needle, placed it in his hand, then went into a semi-trance, staring at it. He began to speak to invisible presences, and told Van Der Post that the spirits would have killed him if they had not known that his intentions — in visiting the Slippery Hills — were pure. Van Der Post suggested that he wrote a letter of apology, which they all signed, and buried in a bottle at the foot of a sacred rock painting; from that moment, the 'jinx' went away. The guide remarked later that the spirits were now far less powerful than they used to be — once they would have killed on sight anyone who had approached so unceremoniously.

The notion of elemental spirits — inhabiting trees or hills — strikes the western mind as totally preposterous. Yet it was not always so. In Ireland — even in Cornwall, where I live — there is still a great deal of belief in fairies and nature spirits in remote country areas. In the 1920s, a psychic named Geoffrey Hodson specialised in describing elementals and nature spirits, and his book about them — entitled, rather off-puttingly, *Fairies at Work and Play* was taken seriously by many people involved in psychical research. (Hodson himself was a Theosophist.) Here is a typical description of what he calls a 'nature deva', encountered in June 1922 when climbing in the Lake District:

'After a scramble of several hundred feet up a rocky glen we turned out to one side, on to the open fell where it faces a high crag. Immediately on reaching the open we became aware, with startling suddenness, of the presence of a great nature-deva, who appeared to be partly within the hillside.

'My first impression was of a huge, brilliant crimson bat-like thing, which fixed a pair of burning eyes upon me.'

'The form was not concentrated into the true human shape, but was somehow spread out like a bat with a human face and eyes, and with wings outstretched on the mountainside. As soon as it felt itself to be observed it flashed into its proper shape, as if to confront us, fixed its piercing eyes upon us, and then sank into the hillside and disappeared. When first seen its aura must have covered several hundred feet of space...'

We find such notions absurd; but they would be accepted by most primitive peoples. From the Eskimos to the Ainus of Northern Japan, from the Orochon of Siberia to the Indians of Tierra del Fuego, the *shaman* is the intermediary between this world and the world of spirits. A man became a *shaman* through painful ordeals, both physical and spiritual. An Eskimo *shaman* told the Danish explorer Rasmussen: 'I could see and hear in a totally different way. I had gained my enlightenment, the *shaman's* light of brain and body, and this in such a manner that it was not only I who could see through the darkness of life, but the same bright light also shone out from me, imperceptible to human beings, but visible to all spirits of earth and sky and sea, and these now came to me as my helping spirits.' The idea of being able to see the world of the spirits 'of earth and sky and sea' can be found in all shamanistic religions.

This curious oneness with nature enables the *shaman* or witch-doctor to exert his power over animals. In *The Occult* I have quoted that amazing passage from Sir Arthur Grimble's book *Pattern of Islands*, describing how a 'porpoise caller' withdrew into his hut for several hours, where he went into a trance; in this trance, apparently, his spirit went out to sea and summoned the porpoises. Finally, he rushed out of the hut calling 'They come, they come'. And to Grimble's astonishment, they *did* come. The villagers waded into the sea and stood breast deep and hundreds of porpoises swam slowly into the beach, apparently in a state of hypnosis, allowing themselves to be beaten to death.

Ross Salmon, a British explorer who spent much of the 1960s and 70s in search of the 'lost world of the Incas', has described in a book called *My Quest For El Dorado* a ceremony among the Callawaya Indians of northern Bolivia which reveals this same intimacy between man and nature. A girl named Wakchu had been accused of being unfaithful to her husband during his absence, and the village elders decided that she would be 'tried' by the condor, the sacred bird of the village, which was believed to embody the spirit of a famous hero. Ross Salmon was given permission to film the whole ceremony. He described, in a television interview accompanying his film, his incredulity at the idea that the priests could summon a condor — a shy bird, which he had never seen at close quarters. Wakchu was tied to a pole at the

top of the cliff, wearing only a loincloth, and the three priests began a ceremony to call the condor, supported by a chorus of women. For half an hour, nothing happened, and Salmon became convinced it was a waste of time. Then, to his amazement, an enormous condor flew overhead, together with two females. It landed near Wakchu, strutted around for a while, then ran ran towards her and pointed its beak at her throat. The villagers murmured 'Guilty'. One of the camera crew threw a stone at the bird, which flew off. Wakchu committed suicide a few days later by throwing herself from a cliff. She evidently accepted the judgement of the condor.*

Another account of life among South American Indians conveys this same sense of intimacy with nature. *Wizard of the Upper Amazon* by F. Bruce Lamb tells the story of Manuel Córdova-Rios, who was kidnapped by the Amahuaca Indians of the Amazon, and who lived among them for many years. Much of their 'magic' was involved with hunting, and apparently worked. Rios witnessed a method of luring pigs. It was important for the hunters to kill the sow who led a band of pigs. Then her head was buried in a hole, facing the opposite direction from which the hunters are travelling. The hole is filled in while the hunters sing chants to the spirits of the forest. If this is done correctly, the pigs will continue to pass over this spot at regular intervals, in the circuit of their territory.

It also seems that the Amahuaca Indians are capable of group telepathy as well as of this kind of direct contact with nature. Clearly, their modes of perception are more 'right brain' than ours. But since we now know that our left-brain perception has been developed by the pressures of civilisation, and that the being who lives in the right is virtually a stranger, there is less reason for dismissing these stories of primitive empathy with nature as old wives tales.

It now becomes possible to understand the ceremonies performed by our Cro-Magnon ancestors before setting out on hunting expeditions, and those cave paintings of *shamans* performing ritual dances and wearing the skins of animals. The purpose is not simply to locate the herd of animals to be hunted the next day *(shamans* should be regarded as mediums rather than magicians), but to somehow *lure* it to a place where the hunters can find it, as Grimble's porpoise caller lured the porpoises.

Recent research has demonstrated fairly convincingly that circles of standing stones like Stonehenge and Avebury were intended as solar and lunar calendars. The discoveries of 'ley hunters' like John Michell seem to suggest that there were also temples for the performance of fertility rituals. But I remain convinced that if we are to understand the real purpose of the standing stones, we have to put ourselves into the state of mind of the Callawayas or Amahuacas, and understand that the ancient priests were probably *shamans* who went into a trance and *conversed* with nature spirits,

*Salmon's version in the book differs in some particulars from his account on Westward Television; I have preferred the television version, which Salmon claims embodies his considered opinion.

19

asking them to guarantee the abundance of the harvest.

Once we begin to understand this, we can also understand the origins of 'witchcraft'. A *shaman* who has the power to converse with 'spirits' to ask them to bless his tribe may also make use of them to revenge himself on an enemy. In *The Occult*, I have described the theory advanced by anthropologist Ivar Lissner about why our ancestors suddenly ceased to make images of human beings. They reasoned that if 'magic' could be used to destroy a reindeer or bear, it could also be used to destroy another human being. So the making of images became taboo — or something carried out in secret by 'black' magicians — what would later be called 'followers of the left hand path'. (It is significant that our ancestors equated the left with the sinister — sinister in Latin means left — while right was synonymous with goodness; they were clearly aware that the two aspects of the human mind are separate, but had no means of knowing that the right half of the brain governs the left half of the body and vice versa.)

Neal's *Ju-ju in My Life* describes his own gradual conversion to belief in the malevolent power of witch-doctors — in this case, through unpleasant personal experience. After causing the arrest of a man who had been extorting bribes from farmers, Neal was told that he had now become the target for ju-ju. On three occasions he found a black powder scattered on the seat of his car, which his chauffeur carefully brushed off, urinating on it to remove the 'spell'. Then Neal became seriously ill — he actually describes an 'out of the body' experience — although the European doctors could not diagnose the illness. A black subordinate offered to call in his uncle, an expert on ju-ju attacks. The uncle performed certain rituals, then described in detail the man who was behind the attacks — a man he had never seen. But the attacks continued. One night, Neal felt himself bitten as he lay in bed, but could find nothing in his bed. Powerful forces seemed to be attacking his solar plexus and draining his vitality. He began to see the creatures that were attacking him — long-snouted things, which he took to be on the astral level. He became seriously ill again. This time, his subordinate brought a Moslem holy man, who asked for three sheep and three bottles of gin, as well as a pound note, which was to be changed into pennies and given to innocent children. This seemed to work, and Neal slowly recovered his strength.

Stories concerning the power of witch-doctors over snakes can be found in *Mitsinari*, an account by Father André Dupreyat of his years in Papua, New Guinea. Father Dupreyat challenged some local sorcerers, and was warned that he was in danger from black magic. One day, about to enter a village, he was surprised to see the villagers scattering. A snake with silvery skin was on the path, rearing towards him. Dupreyat knew it would have to lower its head

20

to wriggle in his direction, so he waited until it did this, then killed it with his stick. The villagers assured him that it had been sent by the sorcerers — which he was unwilling to believe.

The next day while lying in a hut in another village and smoking a pipe, he became aware of the head of a snake a few feet away, hanging from the roof-beam. It dropped on to his chest as he lay still, then wriggled on to the floor, where he was able to kill it with his stick. A few days later there was another 'snake attack', when two black snakes writhed up the support of his hammock; another man in the hut warned him, and he was able to kill them with a knife that was cautiously handed to him. Dupreyat describes the technique the Papuan sorcerers use to persuade snakes to attack their enemies. The snake is placed in a closed vessel with a loin cloth belonging to the intended victim, and left for days until it becomes frantic to escape. It is maddened by blows on the pot and by being heated over a fire, and repeatedly attacks the loincloth in its fury and frustration. Then finally, the pot is placed close to a spot where the intended victim will pass, with a length of liana attached to the lid to release it at the vital moment; at which the maddened snake recognises the smell of the man and attacks him...

These stories of witchcraft and magic among primitive peoples provide us with an insight into the history of witchcraft in Europe. Most modern books on the subject take the view that the 'witchcraft craze' (as the historian Trevor-Roper calls it) was a matter of superstition. The most comprehensive encyclopedia on the subject — by Rossell Hope Robbins — accepts it as a basic premise that witches were simply unfortunate old women who suffered because of the superstitious ignorance and credulity of their neighbours. And indeed, there is some historical truth in this view, for witchcraft began — as we shall see — as a hunt for heresy. But if our primitive ancestors really *could* perform 'magic', then the ancient belief in witchcraft is not merely a matter of superstition. Witches were the descendants of those *shamans* who lured the quarry into the ambush of the hunters, and who later used their magic to ensure a good harvest.

In a book called *Strange Powers* I have explained my own conversion to the view that witchcraft often 'worked'. In the earlier book *The Occult*, I had discussed the case of the North Berwick witches, and accepted Rossel Hope Robbin's view that they were innocent. Yet in *The Occult*, I also cite stories of African witchcraft told to me by Negley Farson and Martin Delany, and accept that these are true. When I re-read the Berwick case, I saw that it has some very puzzling features.

What happened was this. A young maidservant named Gilly Duncan was able to cure various ailments by some form of faith healing. In 1590 her master David Seaton, deputy bailiff of Tranent, near Edinburgh, tortured her with a rope around her neck to make her 'confess' to intercourse with the devil, which eventually she did. She was handed over to the authorities, and soon confessed that her accomplices — about seventy in number — included many highly respectable citizens of Edinburgh, including one Agnes Sampson, an elderly gentlewoman of good education. Under prolonged torture, Agnes Sampson finally confessed — although not until her inquisitors found on her a 'devil's mark' in the area of her vagina. John Fian, a schoolmaster from Saltpans, and two other women, Euphemia Maclean and Barbara Napier, 'reputed for as civil, honest women as any that dwelled within the city of Edinburgh', were also accused. Agnes Sampson now gave a full account of her attempts to bewitch the king — James the Sixth of Scotland (later James the First of England) — who, understandably, took an active interest in the proceedings. Fian confessed under torture, but later managed to escape; when recaptured, he recanted his confession, and the most appalling tortures failed to make him change his mind. He was strangled and burned. Euphemia Maclean was burned without being first strangled — probably because she was a Catholic — but Barbara Napier managed to get her sentence delayed on the grounds that she was pregnant, and finally escaped.

Certainly, this sounds like a case of horrifying injustice. James the First, who wrote a famous *Demonologie*, later decided that most witchcraft was superstition, and persecution of witches almost ceased towards the end of his reign.

Fuller examination of the case raises doubts about their innocence. John Fian had been secretary to the Earl of Bothwell, a man with a reputation for dabbling in black magic, and who had every reason for wanting to kill the king, since he himself was heir to the throne. James was himself sceptical about the confession of Agnes Sampson until — according to the chronicle *Newes from Scotland* — she took him aside and whispered in his ear certain words that had passed between him and his bride, Anne of Denmark, on their wedding night. No one but the king and his bride knew what they were. Naturally, James was convinced.

Agnes Sampson also confessed that she and the others had raised a storm to attempt to drown the King on his way back from Denmark — and indeed, the king *had* almost been drowned in a tremendous storm. She described how she had tied a toad by its back legs, collected the venom that dripped from it in an oyster shell, and kept it until some occasion when she could get hold of some of the king's soiled linen, which would enable her to bewitch him to death, making him feel 'as if he had been lying upon sharp thorns and ends of needles..' The method is reminiscent of the one still used by African witch-doctors.

Fian himself seems to have declared that the devil appeared to him in his cell on the night after his original

confession. Since he had already confessed, he was not under the threat of torture, which again leads to the suspicion that he may not have been as innocent as Robbins assumes.

Montague Summers is, of course, convinced that the witches were guilty as charged. He writes: 'The most celebrated occasion when witches raised a storm was that which played so important a part in the trial of Dr Fian and his coven, 1590–1, when the witches, in order to drown King James and Queen Anne on their voyage from Denmark, "took a cat and christened it," and after they had bound a dismembered corpse to the animal "in the night following the said cat was convayed into the middest of the sea by all these witches, sayling in their riddles or cives . . this doone, then did arise such a tempest in the sea, as a greater hath not been seene".' It all sounds preposterous enough, particularly 'sailing in sieves'; but if African witch-doctors can cause rain—or stop it—then Summers could well be basically correct. There is at least a fifty per cent possibility that Fian was involved in a real witchcraft plot to kill the king; and if witchcraft sometimes works, then we cannot rule out the possibility that Agnes Sampson and her associates really caused the storm which almost wrecked the king's ship.

And what of this statement of Fian that the devil appeared to him? This would seem to brand the confession an invention wrung from him by fear of further torture. Yet again, we should not assume that this is the only possible

explanation. In his book about magic and witchcraft in Brazil *The Flying Cow*, Guy Playfair advances the theory that he himself has come to accept through the study of many cases that 'black magic' involves the conjuring of 'low grade' entities or spirits. And this is, of course, consistent with the view of magic held by witch-doctors and *shamans*. If we are willing to admit, as a possibility, that magic involves non-human entities, then Fian may have believed that he saw—or heard—the devil on the night after his confession. We may reject Summers' view that the devil actually exists as the adversary of God—after all, most of what we call evil can be regarded as stupidity or the outcome of frustration—but there is a certain amount of evidence in physical research for 'mischievous' entities (who, in many cases, seem to be half-witted). 'Evil' spirits may be exhibiting the same kind of stupidity and malevolence as evil human beings.

To accept this possibility does not, of course, mean accepting that all 'black' withcraft involves 'spirits' or demons. That would mean accepting the locigal corollary that all white witchcraft involves angels or benevolent spirits. And this is obviously unnecessary. If it is easy enough to believe that a 'healer' is calling upon unrecognised powers of the unconscious mind, then it is no more difficult to believe that a black witch is doing the same. At the moment, our knowledge of these matters is comparable to, say, the state of

chemistry in the year 1800, before Dalton had stumbled upon the atomic theory. We know just enough to know that one enormous chunk of the jigsaw is missing.

Historically speaking, the oddest thing about witchcraft is that nobody bothered much about it until around the year 1300. An early Church document called the Canon Episcopi denounced the notion that 'certain abandoned women perverted by Satan' really flew through the air at night 'with the pagan goddess Diana' as an absurd delusion or dreams. In practice, local healers and 'wise women' were a common feature of country life. The 'witchcraft craze' began when the Church decided it was time to stamp out a heretical sect called the Cathars — also known as Bogomils, Albigenses and (later) Waldenses. The Cathars were religious 'purists', the mediaeval equivalent of Quakers or Methodists; they denounced the wealth and corruption of the Church and insisted that the only way to get to heaven was by leading a godly life. Understandably, this worried the princes of the Church. The Cathars also believed that everything to do with matter is evil, while everything to do with spirit is good. The world, they said, was created by the devil, and the truly religious man should reject all worldly things. One of the odder beliefs of the Cathars was that since Jesus was wholly good, he could not have possessed a physical body; so they taught that Jesus was a phantom. In 1208, the Pope — Innocent III — declared a crusade against the Cathars — and in particular, against Count Raymond of Toulouse, one of whose squires had assassinated the Papal Legate. In 1209 and 1210, twenty thousand crusaders swept across Languedoc, storming towns and massacring their inhabitants. A monk named Dominic Guzman — later St Dominic — set up the Inquisition in Toulouse in 1229, and his agents went around Languedoc rooting out heresy and burning heretics. Rather like the late Senator Joseph Macarthy, Dominic got carried away by his mission until he saw heretics everywhere. It was easy to distort the Cathar belief that the world was created by the devil into the notion that the Cathars worshipped the devil. But it was another century before a new Pope — the paranoid John XXII, who believed his enemies were plotting to kill him by magic — finally gave the Dominicans his support. The 'witch hunt' now really began: at first in the Pyrenees and the Alps, into whose valleys the remnants of the heretics had retreated. The aim was no longer merely to root out heresy — unsound doctrine — but to destroy the servants of the devil. And during the next four centuries, many thousands of 'witches' were strangled and burned — many of them, perhaps most, undoubtedly innocent. In England, the repeal of the witchcraft act in 1736 put an end to the persecutions; the same thing happened all over Europe. The spirit of science, symbolised by Isaac Newton's *Principia Mathematica*, made

belief in magic seem absurd.

But was the 'witchcraft craze' really smoke without fire? The remark in the Canon Episcopi (dating from about the 4th century AD) about the pagan goddess Diana offers an interesting clue. Why Diana, the Roman moon goddess? Because from the very beginning, the history of magic has been associated with the moon. Diana was also the earth goddess — and therefore the goddess of fertility. This association of witches with Diana can be found throughout the centuries. In the 1880s, an American scholar named Charles Leland became fascinated by the English Gypsies — as George Borrow had been half a century earlier — and became president of the Gypsy Lore Society. In 1886 he went to Florence, continuing his studies of Gypsy magic and lore, and encountered an Italian witch named Maddelena, who told fortunes and sold amulets. He employed Maddalena to gather what traditions she could about the origins of Italian witchcraft, which was known as *la vecchia religione*, the old religion. She finally provided him with a handwritten manuscript called *Aradia*, or the Gospel of the Witches. This tells the story of how the goddess Diana had an incestuous affair with her brother Lucifer, and gave birth to Aradia (or Herodias); it was Aradia who eventually came down to earth and taught men and women the secrets of magic. This, according to the Gospel of the Witches, was because the Church and the aristocracy were treating the poor with such cruelty that Diana felt they needed to be provided with some means of self-defence. That is to say, witchcraft was originally a movement of *social protest*, like the Peasant's Revolt. In his *Witchcraft, Magic and Alchemy* (1931), Grillot de Givry hits upon the same idea:'... it is perfectly logical that certain men ... having seen that God possessed his rich and honoured Church on earth ... should have asked themselves — above all, if they believed that they had a right to complain of God, Who had condemned them to a wretched state of life and denied them worldly goods — why Satan ... should not have his Church also ... why they themselves should not be priests of this demon, who would, perhaps, give them what God did not·deign to give...'

There is every reason to believe that *Aradia* is a genuine document, for there could be no possible reason to forge such a work. It would hardly attract the attention of anyone but a folk-lorist — and, in fact, it went out of print almost immediately. It provides one of the most powerful pieces of evidence that witchcraft was a survival of a pagan cult of the moon and earth goddess — a fertility cult.

During the First World War, an English archaeologist named Margaret Murray was living in Glastonbury when she decided to study the history of witchcraft. Without, apparently, studying *Aradia* (at least, she never mentions it), Margaret Murray reached the conclusion that witchcraft was a survival of a pagan fertility cult. It was her view that the

Right A modern dowser investigating the forces of a monolithic standing stone.

image of the devil — as a horned man with a tail — originated in the hunting rituals of our Cro-Magnon ancestors in which the *shaman* wore the skin of the animal about to be hunted. When man became a farmer rather than a hunter, he directed his magic towards the earth with the object of ensuring a good harvest. These innocent pagan festivals continued down the ages. The Church attempted to stamp them out, partly because they were a pagan survival, partly because of their strong sexual undertones — but in many country areas the 'old religion' was simply blended with the new; dances around a maypole replaced the pagan fertility ceremony with its ritual phallus.

In recent years, Margaret Murray's theory — which was once accepted by most respectable scholars — has been violently attacked, on the grounds that she censored the evidence about witchcraft cults and sabbats to support her theories. And there can be no doubt that her later book *The Divine King in England* (which appeared when she was 94) is wildly eccentric, with its theory that many English kings were members of the 'old religion'. Yet no one who looks impartially at the evidence can doubt that witchcraft was closely bound up with the cult of Diana, and that many of its ceremonies were pagan survivals. In his book *The Roots of Witchcraft*, Michael Harrison mentions that after the Second World War, Professor Geoffrey Webb was given the task of surveying damaged churches, and discovered that many altars of churches built before the Black Death contained stone phalluses. (Scholars have long been puzzled by carvings on many ancient churches showing a crouching woman holding open the lips of her vagina — they are known as Sheila-na-gigs.) Harrison also mentions an event documented in the Bishop's Register of Exeter in the 14th century, which states that the monks of Frithelstick Priory in Devon were caught by the Bishop worshipping a statue of 'the unchaste Diana' in the woods, and made them destroy it. Why 'unchaste' Diana, when she is usually known as the 'queen and huntress, chaste and fair'? Because the Bishop recognised the ceremony for what it was — a fertility ritual.

Amusingly enough, Montague Summers is enraged by the theory of Margaret Murray, and denounces it as imaginative moonshine. He is determined to promote his own view that the witches were genuine heretics, inspired by the devil, and that the church was right to 'stamp out the infection lest the whole of society be corrupted and damned'. As we have seen, there is a great deal to be said for his opinions — even though he takes them to the point of absurdity. He is almost certainly in the right when he attacks Margaret Murray's view that Joan of Arc and Gilles de Rais were priests of the Dianic cult who were sacrificed for their faith

All of which only demonstrates that the subject of witchcraft is far more complicated than at first appears. The

truth seems to be roughly this: the 'old religion' survived from the days of our Cro-Magnon ancestors, and in late Neolithic times led to the construction of stone 'temples' like Avebury, Stonehenge and Carnac. This religion involved the invocation of earth spirits and deities — like Van Der Post's 'spirits of the Slippery Hills'. It managed to co-exist quietly with Christianity in Europe — although the authors of the Canon Episcopi knew about it nearly a thousand years before John XXII made it a crime. Almost certainly, it had nothing to do with the rise of Catharism, whose roots are in Manichaeism and Gnosticism. But the persecution of the Cathars drew the attention of the Church to the Old Religion, with dire results. In fact, one of the first results of the persecution of witches was probably to cause them to band together and take their stand against the doctrines of Christianity. So, to some extent, the church created the heresy it was so determined to destroy. If we can believe *Aradia*, they did worship the devil — or Lucifer, the sun god — as well as his sister Diana. And many of them probably practised ancient forms of magic passed down from palaeolithic times. It was not the Church that stamped out witchcraft — it was Newton and Leibniz and Dalton.

And now, it seems, the wheel has come full circle. As we begin to understand something of the mysterious powers of the human mind — as, for example, an increasing number of people recognise that dowsing actually works — we can also begin to sense something of that magical understanding of the universe possessed by our ancestors. As incredible as it sounds, H.G. Wells and Montague Summers can now be reconciled. No doubt they would have hated the idea; but for the rest of us, it opens fascinating prospects.

CHAPTER 1
Primitive Sorcery

'The earliest known representation of a deity is in the Caverne des Trois Frères in Ariège, and dates to the late Palaeolithic period. The figure is that of a man clothed in the skin of a stag and wearing on his head the antlers of a stag.' So says Margaret Murray in the first paragraph of *The God of the Witches*. We know she was fairly certainly wrong; the figure is not a 'deity', but a *shaman* or a sorcerer dressed for the ritual luring of animals before a hunt. But she *is* probably correct when she says that figures like this were the origin of the Christian Devil — and the Greek nature god Pan.

In 1963, a science writer named Alexander Marshack sat at his desk and stared at a photograph of an 8,500 year old bone from Ishango, on the Nile. It was covered with 'scratches' or marks, and an academic article that accompanied it suggested that the prehistoric man who made it was playing some kind of arithmetical game. Marshack felt this was wrong. As it happened, he was writing a book about the moon, and he found himself wondering if these notations could have something to do with it. In fifteen minutes he felt he had 'cracked the code' of the bone. The marks were made in such a way that it constitued a *lunar calendar* with its own inbuilt corrections.

He tried out his theory with even older pieces of marked bone, including one from the Dordogne covered with dot marks in a winding pattern — this was perhaps twenty

thousand years old, made by one of our Cro-Magnon
ancestors. Again, his mathematics convinced him that the
marks were basically a lunar calendar, and that the shape of
the 'dots' showed various phases of the moon. It was, in
effect, the earliest writing.

His epoch-making book *The Roots of Civilisation,* in
which he describes his careful research into many other
artifacts, is still ignored by many scientists — his views seem

too far-fetched. For, after all, what would primitive stone age hunters be doing making such careful notations of the rising and setting of the moon? Why on earth should they *need* them?

In the 1960s, Professor Gerald Hawkins caused equally sceptical reactions when he published an article in *Nature* arguing that Stonehenge is basically a solar and lunar calendar — he based his conclusions on computer analysis of the stones. By the time the earliest part of Stonehenge was constructed — about 2,900 BC, our ancestors had become farmers; so it could be argued that they had some practical use for a calender. But surely nothing as massive and elaborate as Stonehenge? Yet the even more elaborate researches of Professor Alexander Thom seemed to confirm that most — probably all — stone circles serve this same function as calendars. But why so many?

The answer to these questions can only be suggested here. The moon affects the tides. It also causes changes in the earth's magnetic field. Birds and animals use this field for their migrations and for 'homing', and evidence presented by Professor Robin Baker of Manchester now suggests that man is also sensitive to these forces and can 'navigate' with them. Dowsers sense unusual concentrations of this magnetic force in areas such as Stonehenge, often in spiral patterns. (And a spiral motif seems to be found in primitive carvings all over the world.)

Primitive man recognised these forces, and he sensed the way that they are affected by the moon, the sun and the planets. It was this sense of a magical relationship between the earth and the solar system that led to his early interest in the heavens. He also believed — rightly or wrongly — that the earth is permeated with spirit forces, and that these can also be propitiated and used by human beings. So the chief task of the primitive witch or *shaman* was to form a bridge between the human, visible world, and this invisible world of spirits and heavenly forces.

In most ancient cultures the moon was the goddess of magic. And, significantly, she was also the earth goddess. In Greek mythology, Selene the moon goddess blends into Demeter, the earth goddess; Astarte, the Canaanite moon goddess is also the earth goddess. (The planet Venus also blends into these identifications, possibly because it was, next to the moon, the strongest influence on the earth's field.)

What precisely did the ancient priests *do* at Stonehenge or Avebury, or even older circles? Let us confess frankly that the answer is: we have no idea. Modern primitive ceremonies to propitiate the earth spirits may offer us the likeliest clue. But stories of ju-ju (some of them cited in the Introduction) should remind us that we are not speaking simply of some pagan religion, the ancient equivalent of a modern Church of England service. Some strange and often violent reaction between man and nature lay at the heart of these rituals.

CHAPTER 2
The Coming of The Witches

Why did the performance of magic pass from the male *shaman* to the female witch? The likeliest answer is that as man taught himself the arts of agriculture, life became more settled, and the *shaman* no longer had to perform his hunting magic. Says Jacob Grimm in his *Teutonic Mythology:* 'To woman, not to man, was assigned the culling and concocting of powerful remedies, as well as the cooking of food...The restless lives of men were filled up with war, hunting, agriculture and handicrafts; to women experience and convenient leisure lent every qualification for secret sorcery. Woman's imagination is warmer and more susceptible, and at all times an inner sacred power of divination was revered in her..'

Long before Margaret Murray, indeed, half a century before Leland's *Aradia,* Grimm realised that witch ceremonies are derived from pagan festivals; he mentions Walpurgis Night (May 1) as a 'grand annual excursion of witches', pointing out that it is the 'date of a sacrificial feast and the old May-gathering of the people'. 'To Christian zealots all dancing appears sinful ... and sure enough it often was derived from pagan rites, like other harmless pleasures and customs...Hence the old dancings at Shrovetide, at the Easter Fire and May Fire..' 'The witches invariably resort to places where formerly justice was administered, or sacrifices were offered..'And he adds that many 'conjuring spells' have

nothing to do with the devil, but far more often refer to the 'elvish' — to nature spirits. So, with the instinct of a lifelong student of folklore, Grimm concludes that the real essence of witchcraft is 'milder' and more pagan than Christian zealots recognise.

In fact, the world of the witches, as it emerges in Grimm's researches, is the world of elves and fairies, of woodlands and mountain-tops and ancient sacred places, not of blasphemous rituals and invocations of the powers of hell.

CHAPTER 3
The Left Hand Path

It must have been a temptation to the Stone Age *shaman* to use his power to get his own way, or to revenge insults. As Tolkien's Gandalf remarks: 'Wizards are impatient and quick to anger'.

But to use his powers for personal ends raises certain problems for the magician. The 'you', the personality, lives in the left-brain. The 'non-you' lives in the right, the unconscious. This is the source of creativity, of what Keats called 'negative capability'. Gurdjieff called it 'essence'. And the non-you is almost certainly the source of magical powers. To use these for left-brain purposes is to risk cutting them off at the source.

In that case, 'black magic' ought to be impossible — or at least, self-defeating, gradually depleting the powers of the magician. Why is this not so? Because, according to the world-wide magical tradition, the black magician can make use of low-grade spirits to carry out his bidding.

In doing so, he (or she) is not being wicked so much as stupid. He is foregoing real power for the satisfaction of the ego.

Real magic — the 'right hand path' — depends on learning to use the 'true will', which seems to reside in the right. (At least, the right is the gateway to it.) In that sense, black magic is a counterfeit, a deceit.

However, men being what they are, the left hand path

was bound to flourish. One of the most frequently used methods of magic was the making of images, usually of wax. An early Egyptian manuscript — the Westcar Papyrus (about 2700 BC) — tells how the king's steward destroyed his wife's lover by making a wax crocodile, 'seven spans long', which turned into a real crocodile when the lover came down to bathe and killed him. But it was far more common to model the intended victim — or sometimes only the heart — in wax, and then to drive needles into the figure or melt it. The making of figurines is the oldest of all magical practices.

The earliest magic was hunting magic, and the stone age drawings of animals in caves were not intended as artistic representations but as magical images intended to influence the actual animals.

When man became an agriculturalist, the magic of the priests was now directed at ensuring a good harvest. Inevitably, then, it was sometimes used for the opposite purpose — to blast the harvest of enemies. Because toads were believed to be poisonous, they were sometimes used in these ceremonies. (Charles Walton, the victim of the 'witchcraft murder' at Lower Quinton (Warwickshire) in 1945 is reported to have harnessed toads to a toy plough and made them run across the fields.)

The notion of black magic, the left hand path, seems to emerge fairly late in history. Persia is the traditional home of

Right Charles Walton bewitching crops with toads harnessed to a toy plough.

magic; but the Magi were priests, the wise men of the Bible. The Greeks regarded Egypt as the land of magic; yet there were no specifically 'black' witches or magicians in ancient Egypt. The legendary Circe, daughter of the sun god and sea nymph, could change men into swine; yet Homer does not seem to regard her as wicked; she was an enchantress, not a witch.

What seems to have happened is that with the coming of civilisation, the *shamans* and witches no longer had a specific job to do—except those that became priests or priestesses. The rest had to retire into private life. And the official priests no doubt regarded them as a nuisance. The Biblical King Saul—around 1000 BC—issued an edict against witchcraft; but according to the First Book of Samuel, he had to call upon the services of the Witch of Endor in order to consult the deceased King Samuel to find out why the Lord had ceased to regard him with favour.

In the *Odyssey*, Odysseus summons the spirits of the dead through a ceremony involving sacrifice—he wants to consult the shade of the seer Tiresias. Homer was writing about two centuries after King Saul, in the beginning of the eighth century BC. Towards the end of the same century, another Greek poet, Hesiod, makes the first reference to Hecate, the goddess of the underworld and of the moon—that is, of magic. This combination of functions also explains why the magical art later became known as necromancy—the art of communication with the dead.

CHAPTER 4

The Earliest Witches

Circe was not a witch in the modern sense of the word; she was an enchantress. But the modern notion of a witch — an evil old hag with supernatural powers — enters world mythology long before the coming of Christianity. The Greek orator Demosthenes, writing around 350 BC, mentions that a woman named Theoris of Lemnos had been tried as a witch in Athens and burned. It seems typical that she should be condemned by the city that had sentenced Socrates to death.

What happened, of course, is that city-dwellers created their own exaggerated image of witchcraft. Country people, living in contact with the local 'wise man' or woman, know that a witch is a useful member of the community. Town-dwellers, no longer in contact with nature, invent preposterous stories of magic and malevolence. And this is not just because they are credulous, but also because they are incredulous; half the time they believe that magic is nonsense; the other half, they believe it is frightening and dangerous. Both attitudes spring out of a lack of acquaintance with the real thing.

Around 300 BC, the Greek poet Theocritus writes of a girl named Samaetha, who prays to Hecate and performs a magical ceremony on the seashore to bring back her faithless lover. Basically, she is only performing a religious ceremony. But over the next two or three centuries, the image of the witch changes. And when the Roman poet Horace writes about two witches named Canidia and Sagana, they are horrible crones, 'pale of face, barefooted, their hair dishevelled', who gather poisonous herbs in the graveyard and tear a black lamb to pieces with their bare hands. They make a wax image of their victim, then invoke the goddess of Hell — Hecate — and the Furies. 'Snakes and hounds of Hell appear. Ghosts utter shrill, forlorn cries, and the waxen image, thrown into the fire, flares up brightly.'

In fact, the witch as she appears in Ovid, Horace, Lucan, Petronius, Lucius Apuleius, is as unreal and as absurd as a genie out of the *Arabian Nights*.

The greatest of all novels about witchcraft, *The Golden Ass* by Lucius Apuleius, resembles the *Arabian Nights* in more ways than one. It begins with a story told by a traveller about how a friend of his had offended a witch. In the middle of the night, witches burst into their bedroom, and cut the man's throat, then they tear out his heart, and replace it with a sponge. As they walk out the door locks itself behind them. Yet the next morning, the victim seems in perfectly good health — until he tries drinking from a stream, at which the wound in his throat opens up and he falls down dead...

Lucius goes on to describe how he goes to stay in the house of a moneylender named Milo, whose wife is a witch. One night he peers through a crack in the door and watches the witch smearing herself with an ointment that transforms her into an owl. Anxious to try it out, Lucius persuades the serving maid who was also his mistress to smear him with ointment — and finds himself changed into an ass. The remainder of the novel is about his comic adventures as he tries to find a bunch of roses, the taste of which will restore him to his proper form. He endures various mishaps and adventures until finally the moon goddess — Isis — intervenes to save him (the cult of Isis had been brought to Rome from Egypt — she was identified with Diana and the Greek Selene). Lucius is transformed back into a man, and becomes a votary of the goddess, devoting his life to her service — as Apuleius himself did.

In these last chapters of the book, it is clear that Apuleius is making a serious point. He addresses the moon goddess as 'blessed Queen of Heaven, whether you are pleased to be known as Ceres (the earth goddess).. or whether as celestial Venus.. or whether as Artemis, the physician sister of Phoebus (the sun god)..' Artemis is the Greek version of the Roman Diana, the 'queen and huntress, chaste and fair'. Lucius's 'sin' is his romantic interest in witchcraft — the 'left hand path', and the lesson is that, if he is interested in magic, he should follow the right hand path of devotion to the moon goddess and her mystery religion. The point is as valid today as it was in the second century AD.

CHAPTER 5
The Devil

The witch persecutions would have been impossible without the idea of the Devil, and the Devil was basically the invention of Christian theologians.

Readers who recall Satan in the Book of Job, or the fall of Lucifer, son of the morning, in Isaiah, may feel this is an exaggeration. But Isaiah was not referring to a rebel angel, but to the King of Babylon; and the Accuser in the Book of Job is not Satan but *a* satan, the Hebrew word meaning an adversary or obstructor. When the Old Testament was translated into Greek, 'satan' became 'diabolos' — again, meaning adversary — and this eventually became the Christian Devil.

In this sense, the Devil can be traced back to St Paul. It was St Paul who invented the Vicarious Atonement, the notion that man had fallen from divine grace through the sin of Adam, tempted by the Devil, (although there is no suggestion in the Old Testament that the serpent was anything but an ordinary snake); and the death of Jesus on the cross had offered man a chance of redemption. (Jesus himself never made any such suggestion.) If there is a Christ, there must also be an Antichrist.

Even so, the Devil who tempts Jesus in the wilderness in Matthew is a development of the 'satan' in Job rather than the later Christian Devil; the satan in Job had been 'walking up and down the earth', and Jesus's Devil is the 'lord of this world.'

It is difficult for an unbiased historian to feel anything but irritation when writing about the early history of the Christian Church. It is true that while they were being persecuted by the Romans, Christians showed themselves at their greatest; but as soon as Christianity began to gain the upper hand, after Constantine, they behaved like barbarians, destroying books and works of art, persecuting their pagan enemies, and burning one another for heresy. The council summoned by Constantine at Nicaea in 325 AD promptly began to quarrel about the Trinity, and rejected the commonsense view of Arius that Jesus had been created like any other man in favour of the view of Athanasius that he was God. In 381, a council summoned by Theodosius I forbade heretics to assemble and took away their right to inherit prophecy. Fifty years later, Theodosius II instituted the sentence of death on heretics. Monasticism flourished, and the monks and hermits vied with one another in castigating the flesh. Sexual temptation was regarded as the great sin. The emphasis upon sin — every possible form of sin — meant emphasis on the Devil. Theophilus of Alexandria even denounced the saintly (if intolerant) John Chrsostom as 'Satan disguised as an angel of light'. So Christianity became a dark and morbid religion, obsessed with sin and evil, grimly literal-minded about the road to salvation. R.W. Southern remarks in the second volume of *The Pelican History of Christianity:* 'There was a further ultimate impotence that prevented the mediaeval church state from becoming a police-state. It had no police.' It is a sad comment on what had become of Jesus's religion of love and forgiveness.

The lives of saints are full of stories of demons and of the Devil. The Devil tempts St Anthony by appearing to him as a beautiful woman. (They became known as succubi.) In

other accounts he is a fly, a toad, an imp, a black man, a gargoyle, a rat, a horrible stench, a tree, a giant cat, and an incubus whose penis was like an icicle and whose semen made a woman cold inside. And Christians took these stories quite literally; they believed the Devil walked among them, and that they were surrounded by legions of unseen demons. Even as late as 1801, Francis Barrett's book *The Magus* contains two chapters devoted to demons, who are classified into nine orders or degrees, beginning with false gods and ending with tempters; they have names like Asmodeus, Ashtoreth, Belphegor, Amduscias, Abaddon, Agares, Narbas, Glasybolos, Choronzon, Haussibut, and literally thousands of others. (A later demonologist, John Wier, says there are over seven million.)

This crude, literal-minded obsession with evil was increased by the various practical problems of the Church in the Dark Ages. The Arabs invaded Spain; hordes of pagan barbarians swept across Europe; and the Greek Orthodox Church formed a powerful rival to Rome. Then, after about 1100, things began to improve. The Arabs were now on the defensive. European trade was expanding; so was the power of the Church. The only cloud on the horizon was the growth of various dangerous heresies, like Catharism. The Cathars — like Martin Luther a few centuries later — felt the Church was growing too fat and self-indulgent. They wanted to re-spiritualise Christianity. The Church reacted by declaring a Crusade against them in 1208, and announcing that the slaughter of Cathars would not be any hindrance to salvation. When the Crusaders burst into Beziers in July 1209, someone asked the Papal Legate how heretics should be distinguished from true believers; he replied: 'Kill them all; God will look after his own.' So twenty thousand people were slaughtered.

CHAPTER 6

Erichto The Witch

The most famous witch of classical times is Erichtho, the Thessalian witch. (Thessaly, in Greece, was the legendary home of witches.) She is described in a famous episode of the *Pharsalia*, an epic by the Roman poet Lucan (1st century AD) about the war between Caesar and Pompey. Whether Erichtho really existed is uncertain; but Lucan's portrait is typical of the Roman idea of the witch as an evil hag, 'foul with filthiness...her dreadful visage laden with uncombed locks. She destroys crops, digs up graves, and performs gruesome ceremonies' — in fact, she is a female bogey, an 'archetype' like Dracula.

In the *Pharsalia*, Pompey's 'degenerate' son Sextus goes to ask her to show him the future. She explains that she needs a corpse whose speech organs are still intact and flexible. They visit a battlefield and she selects a corpse, which she drags off with a hook through the jaw. Then, with horrible ceremonies, involving the froth of a mad dog, entrails of a lynx, marrow of a stag that has been fed on serpents (Lucan seemed unaware that stags are vegetarians); and incantations to Hecate, the corpse comes to life, and prophesies that Pompey will soon join other heroes in the 'shades'. Then Erichtho performs spells to enable the corpse to die again, and burns the body. The story is crude and preposterous, but may be regarded as a typical example of the popular conception of a witch in late classical times.

CHAPTER 7

Merlin and Morgan le Fay

The real King Arthur was an Anglo-Roman general who defended England against the invading Saxons in the 6th century AD; at his last great battle against them, he inflicted such tremendous losses that they halted to lick their wounds for half a century. General Artorius (his Romanised name) then found that he had given his own people — the Celts — time to quarrel amongst themselves, and he finally died, about 537 AD, after a battle against his own nephew Mordred. Legend has it that his body was taken to Glastonbury, where his half-sister, the enchantress Morgan le Fay (Morgan the Fairy) tried — unsuccessfully — to cure his wounds. The legend of Arthur's burial at Glastonbury persisted down the centuries, strengthened by a belief that he would one day return and drive all foreigners out of England. In 1190, the monks of Glastonbury Abbey dug down between two marble crosses in the Abbey grounds, and found, at a depth of sixteen feet, an enormous coffin containing the skeletons of a man and a woman. A leaden cross above the coffin declared that this was the burial place of King Arthur in the Isle of Avalon. The smaller skeleton, that of a woman, may have been his queen Guinevere.

Within a century of his death, there were many legends about King Arthur, mostly originating in Wales (where many of the Celts had been driven by the Saxons after Arthur's death). They are equally widespread in Cornwall;

and a standing stone near Fowey carries an inscription: 'Here lies Tristan, son of Cunomorus', Cunomorus being the Celtic name for King Mark. This is one of the few genuine historical links with Arthurian legend.

The earliest of the Arthurian tales is the Welsh *Culhwch and Olwen,* dating from the 10th century; it describes how Arthur and his knights helped his cousin Culhwch to perform various tasks set by a giant, and so win the hand of Olwen. There is no mention of Merlin or Morgan le Fay here. Both owe their existence as figures of legend to a Welsh bishop named Geoffrey of Monmouth, writing in the middle of the 13th century. In his *History of the Kings of Britain,* Arthur is turned into a kind of British Alexander the Great. According to Geoffrey, King Uther Pendragon — a real person whose life overlapped that of Arthur — fell in love with Igrain, wife of Gorlois, the Duke of Cornwall, who lived in Tintagel Castle. (In fact, Tintagel Castle was not started until a century before Geoffrey; in Arthur's day there was only a hermitage on the site.) Through the magic of the wizard Merlin, Uther was made to resemble Gorlois, and spent a night with Igrain while her husband was away; as a result, Arthur was conceived. Gorlois was later killed in battle, and Uther married Igrain.

Who was Merlin? It seems that he really existed at about the same time as Arthur. His name was actually Myrddin (Geoffrey changed it to Merlin to avoid it sounding like the French *merde*), and he was a northern British bard and prophet, who served a chief called Gwenddolau; when Gwenddolau was killed in battle in Cumbria, Myrddin went mad and fled to the woods, where he lived as a wild man for several years and gained the power of foretelling the future. Arthur himself moved around the British Isles a great deal — his last battle, Camlan, was fought near Hadrian's Wall — so it is conceivable that there was some association between Arthur and the prophet Myrddin.

According to Geoffrey of Monmouth, writing seven hundred years after the real Myrddin, Merlin was born to a Welsh nun who had been visited in her sleep by an incubus. His birthplace, Carmarthen, was named after him. (Caer Myrddin — Merlin's Fort.) The demon who fathered him intended him to be an Antichrist; this intention was frustrated by the teaching of the good nuns, and Merlin only inherited his father's magical power. As a boy, Merlin is discovered by King Vortigern — the predecessor of Uther Pendragon, who invited the Saxons into England — and helps him to build a tower on Snowdon, prophesying the coming of Arthur, who would defeat the Saxons. Geoffrey also describes how Merlin moved the great stones of Stonehenge from Ireland — where they were known as the Giant's Dance — to Salisbury Plain, by magic. In his later *Life of Merlin,* a poem, Geoffrey of Monmouth borrows more details from the real Myrddin, including the episode of

living as a wild man of the woods in the forests of Caledonia. It is Merlin who suggests to Uther Pendragon that he should have a round table constructed, with a special place for the future hero who will win the Holy Grail. He also predicts the coming of a hero who will drive back the Saxons.

Morgan le Fay, Arthur's wicked half-sister, first appears in a twelfth century poem by Robert de Boron, of which only a fragment survives; she is the ruler of a Fortunate Isle called Avalon, the Isle of Apples — later identified with Glastonbury. This is the form in which she appears in the *Life of Merlin* poem by Geoffrey of Monmouth. In later Arthurian legends, she steadily becomes more evil — Arthur's relentless enemy. In its finalised version, Morgan le Fay is the youngest daughter of Gorlois and Igrain, and therefore Arthur's half-sister. She also has an elder sister, Morgause, with whom Arthur unknowingly commits incest when she comes to his court. In *King Arthur and the Grail*, Richard Cavendish speculates that some missing fragment of the legend tells of Morgan falling in love with Arthur. And in fact, such an episode seems to be necessary to make sense of the rest of the story — her hatred of Arthur and of Queen Guinevere and her plots against them.

The legend tells how Morgan was schooled in a convent, then came to Arthur's court. Merlin fell in love with her, and taught her the arts of magic when she promised to give herself to him — she failed to keep her promise. But she took many other lovers, finally marrying a King Urien. At one point she stole the sword Excalibur, substituting a skilful imitation, then lured Arthur into a fight with her lover Accolon of Gaul, who had the real Excalibur. The intervention of another enchantress, the Lady of the Lake, caused Accolon to drop his sword, and Arthur seized it and won the battle. Supporting the notion that Morgan's hostility to Arthur was based on incestuous passion is the legend that she tried to save his life by tending his wounds at Glastonbury, after his final battle, and took away his body in a boat.

Merlin himself finally succumbed to the charms of an enchantress called Viviane, who — like Morgan — persuaded him to teach her magic by promising to give herself, then imprisoned him in a castle made of mist, where he died.

The real significance of these tales of magic is that, like Lucan's evil witch Erichtho, they seem to satisfy a basic hunger of the imagination - that is, they are what Jung calls an archetype. The wicked queen in *Snow White* is a later version of the Morgan archetype, while Tolkien's Gandalf is, in all essentials, Merlin. The dragon — which appears so frequently in Arthurian legends — is another archetype, whose current incarnation is probably the Loch Ness monster.

The significance of the archetypes is that they appear in so many different forms; when one dies out, another takes its place. The witch is another basic archetype.

The Lady of the Lake.

CHAPTER 8
The Destruction of The Templars

When Jacques de Molay, Grand Master of the Knights Templar, was slowly burned to death on an island in the Seine in 1314, he summoned the Pope and the King to 'meet him within a year before the throne of God'. Oddly enough, both men — the two most responsible for the downfall of the Templars — died within a year.

The Knights Templar were among the first — and most distinguished — victims of the witchcraft craze. In 1118, after the First Crusade had opened the Holy Land to Christian Pilgrims, a knight called Hugues de Payens conceived the apparently absurd notion of guarding and policing the roads of the Holy Land with a band of eight knights. This preposterous idea appealed to the King of Jerusalem, who granted them a wing of the palace that had once been Solomon's temple. Their monastic discipline soon turned the Templars into a formidable fighting force. Hugues deliberately sought out knights who had been excommunicated, and so felt they had nothing to lose. Grateful crusaders often bequeathed the Templars their land or possessions, and the Order soon became wealthy. In fact, they became the chief bankers of the Holy Land — even the Moslems banked with them because they were famous for their honesty.

The Order had its ups and downs — in 1187 the Templars were massacred by Saladin, and the Grand Master, Gerard de Ridfort, ordered the remaining Templar garrisons to surrender. But the Templars soon regained their power and wealth — partly as a result of a compromise with their Moslem enemies. In 1244 they regained Jerusalem — not by battle, but by negotiation. But in the same year they were again almost wiped out, this time by an Egyptian army.

Yet again they recovered; but the Mongols under Genghis Khan and the Egyptians under Baybars kept up unrelenting pressure. By 1303, they had been driven out of the Holy Land, to take refuge in Cyprus.

But they were still immensely rich. Philip IV of France resented their power and their wealth; but since he was practically bankrupt, he had to borrow from them. The ideal would clearly be to destroy them and seize their wealth. But how? The obvious answer was: accuse them of heresy and intercourse with the Devil. In that case, their lands and possessions would be forfeited.

Secret orders went out, and at daybreak on 13 October 1307, the authorities swooped and arrested almost every Templar in France.

An ex-Templar had provided the accusations: homosexuality (which is probably the only one with any foundation in fact), intercourse with a demon named Baphomet (who was worshipped in the form of a wooden penis and a jewelled skull) and spitting on the cross. It was alleged that everyone who became a Templar had to become a sodomite, and that the initiation ceremony including kissing the mouth, navel and anus of his sponsor. The ceremonies to Baphomet took place in front of young virgins and female demons.

The knights were tortured so brutally that thirty six of them died within days of their arrest. In November that year (1307) Pope Clement V, a sick weakling, issued a Bull ordering all kings to arrest Templars. At this stage, no one could afford to allow the Templars to regain their power. For three years, Templars were tortured, and in 1310, 54 of them were burned to death, all refusing to confess to the charges of devil-worship. By 1312, the Pope had to reluctantly admit that the charge of heresy would not stand up; but he dissolved the order.

Jacques de Molay *had* confessed under horrible tortures, and was sentenced to life imprisonment. Exposed in public before Notre Dame to make a confession, he dismayed everyone by declaring that his only offence was to lie under torture, and that the Order was innocent. The following day, at sunset, he was burned alive on a slow fire.

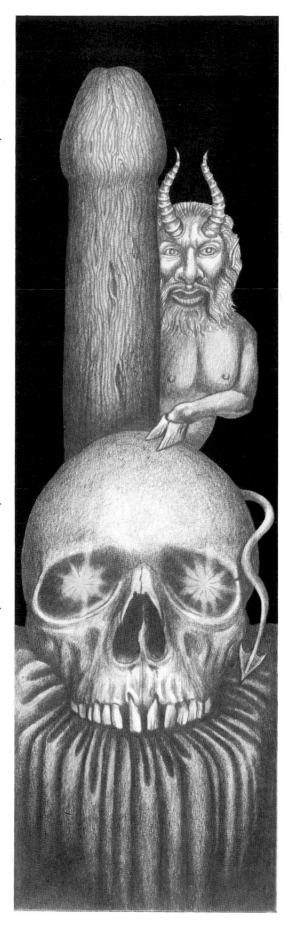

CHAPTER 9

The First Witch Trial

In 1275, a sixty year old woman named Angéle de la Barthe was tried before the Inquisitor Hugues de Baniols at Toulouse. The prime charge was of heresy (Toulouse had been the centre of heresy); but she was also charged with having had sexual intercourse with a demon, and given birth to a monster. This creature had to be fed on the flesh of dead babies, so Angéle either murdered children, or dug up their corpses from graveyards. The confession was undoubtedly obtained from her by torture. Angéle de la Barthe was sentenced to be burned to death.

CHAPTER 10

Jehanne de Brigue

The first secular trial for witchcraft — as distinguished from heresy — took place in Paris in 1390.

The oddity of the case of Jehanne de Brigue is that she *was* probably guilty of practising 'sorcery'. The case against her was brought by a man called Jehane de Ruilly — whose complaint seems to have been that Jehanne saved his life by witchcraft. He had been so ill that he had been given only a week to live. He consulted Jehanne de Brigue, who had a reputation as a witch — in fact, she had been jailed for it at Meaux. Jehanne told him that he had been 'hexed' (or bewitched) by his ex-mistress Gilete, who had borne him two children. However, Jehanne's 'charms' — making a waxen figure of Gilete, and suckling two toads — apparently worked, and Ruilly recovered.

Jehanne at first denied being a witch, but after three months in prison, admitted that she had learned witchcraft from her aunt, who had taught her to summon a demon called Haussibut. She had cured Ruilly, she said, with the help of Haussibut. The court sentenced her to death, but delayed the sentence because she was pregnant. Jehanne decided to appeal to the Parlement of Paris.

The Parlement — consisting of twelve men — was less sympathetic than she had hoped, and suggested that she should be 'put to the torture'. Hereupon, Jehanne confessed that the whole affair had been inspired by Ruilly's wife

Macette, who hated him because he beat her. According to Jehanne, Ruilly had sickened because he was being poisoned by a 'philtre' concocted by her and Macette; they had also made a waxen image of him and presumably stuck pins in it or performed other black magic ceremonies.

Macette at first denied everything; but after being placed on the rack, decided to confess. On August 11, 1391, both women were led to the Chatelet aux Halles, where mitres were placed on their heads as a sign that they were sorcerers; then both were led to the pig market, where they were to be burned alive. However, there were still further doubts and consultations. Lawyers argued that since no one had died, the death sentence was too harsh. But at a supplementary hearing, Ruilly declared that his page had recently killed two toads in the courtyard of his house. This was regarded as clinching evidence. On August 19th, 1391, both women were burned to death.

Were Jehanne and Macette guilty as charged? The chief problem in all witchcraft cases is that confessions under torture, or threat of torture, are valueless as evidence. Rossell Hope Robbins quotes a moving letter from Johannes Junius, burgomaster of Bamberg, accused of witchcraft in 1628, to his daughter Veronica. '..the executioner put the thumb-screw on me so that the blood spurted from the nails...so that for four weeks I could not use my hands..' The executioner himself finally said: 'Sir, I beg you for God's sake confess something, whether it be true or not.. One torture will follow another until you say you are a witch..' He was forced to invent absurdities about a Sabbat and about plotting to kill his children. When his invention dried up they proposed to subject him to the strappado in which the hands are bound behind the back and the victim hauled into the air by a rope around his wrists, so the shoulder joints are twisted. They proposed to push Junius off a ladder in this position, so his arms would have become dislocated; so he invented more absurdities. The letter ends: 'Good night, for your father Johannes Junius will never see you more.'

Jehanne de Brigue was also, at one point, stripped naked and tied to a ladder; it was this that led her to implicate Macette. So the whole involvement of Macette is suspect. It does seem likely that Jehanne *was* practising some kind of witchcraft against Ruilly, and that he suspected as much, which explains why he accused her in the first place. (After all, he otherwise had no reason, since she had 'cured' him.)

So the case of Jehanne de Brigue illustrates the difficulty encountered by a modern commentator in understanding the 'witchcraft craze'. But we can justly accuse the Parlement of Paris of *over-reacting* to Jehanne de Brigue's misdemeanours. It is clear that this over-reaction caused the death of thousands of innocent people, like Johannes Junius. But let this not blind us to the fact that the Church was reacting to a *reality,* and not to a pure delusion.

CHAPTER 11
The Malleus Maleficarum

The most influential book on witchcraft was the work of two Dominicans; it did more to fan the flames of witch hysteria than any other single work. Jacob Sprenger was Dean of Cologne University, and Heinrich Kramer was the Prior of a monastery. Their book *Malleus Maleficarum* means *Hammer of Witches*. Montague Summers calls it 'one of the most important, wisest and weightiest books of the world'. Rossell Hope Robbins calls it 'the most important and most sinister work on demonology ever written'. The truth lies between the two.

In spite of Pope John XXII's bull *Super illius specula* in 1326, which allowed Inquisitors to treat witchcraft itself as a crime (instead of heresy), the witch persecutions started off slowly. In 1459-60, the Inquisitors accused various people of Arras, in northern France of witchcraft and heresy, torturing a weak minded woman named Deniselle Grenières to make her name accomplices. Deniselle and four people she named were burned alive; but when the Inquisitors went on to arrest and torture others, commonsense prevailed, and the Archbishop of Rheims and two bishops declared the whole thing to be an illusion, and the Parlement of Paris ordered the release of the suspects — most of whom had been tortured. This was also a triumph for the views of the Canon Episcopi which declared witchcraft an illusion. In Germany also, witchcraft persecution was sporadic and brief.

Pope Innocent VIII, who came to the papal throne in 1484, was deeply disturbed by this general disbelief in witches. He admired Heinrich Kramer who had been Inquisitor for Tyrol, Salzburg, Bohemia and Moravia since 1474, and who had written an influential tract on witchcraft. So one of the first things Innocent did on becoming Pope was to issue a bull *Summis desiderantes affectibus* ('desiring with the most profound anxiety') which denounced those 'who have abandoned themselves to demons, incubi and succubi' and praised 'our dear sons Heinrich Kramer and James Sprenger' for trying to stamp out this evil. This was in 1484, two years later there appeared the first edition of the huge tract *Malleus Maleficarum*, discussing witchcraft at enormous length and explaining how it could be combated. No doubt its questions about sexual matters made it one of the most widely read books of its time. '..the foulest venereal acts are performed by such devils, not for the sake of pleasure, but for the pollution of the souls and bodies of those to whom they act as incubi and succubi'. Demons can have sexual intercourse with witches, but the semen with which they pollute them is received from another (presumably a male witch). There is a learned discussion as to whether witches can cause a man's penis to disappear. Understandably, this piquant combination of sex and demonology went into several editions and many languages. Significantly, it mentions that witches worship Diana and Herodias, and says that incubi are satyrs, called Pans in Greek. The Church clearly suspected that witchcraft was a pagan cult.

The invention of printing turned the *Hammer of Witches* into the first best-seller, and spread the witch hysteria across Europe.

Young witch being visited by an incubus.

62

CHAPTER 12
Magic and Magicians

Very close to the witchcraft tradition, yet clearly separated from it, is the ancient tradition of natural magic. This tradition undergoes certain fundamental changes after the appearance of the *Zohar,* or Book of Splendour, around 1300; thereafter it becomes specifically 'cabbalistic' (based on the Kabbalah).

Magic may be defined as man's discovery of the peculiar powers of his own mind, and the recognition that his mental efforts could influence reality. The *shamans* who drew images of wild animals on the walls of caves believed that their ceremonies could influence the hunt. We may regard this simply as a manifestation of early man's religious impulse, in which he asked the gods to help the hunters. But anyone who knows something about modern African witchcraft and sorcery, or the voodoo of Haiti and Brazil, may feel that it was not entirely a matter of superstition; there is a great deal of evidence that magic 'works'. At the moment we are in no position to know how it works, since there are two major unknown factors: the powers of the unconscious mind, and the hidden forces of nature. When a dowser's rod responds to underground water — or to standing stones — a part of his mind is responding to forces that have so far remained unidentified by science. When a 'psychometrist' holds a letter, or some other object, in his hand, and is able to describe the person to whom it belongs, he is apparently picking up some kind of recording, whose nature is probably similar to that of an ordinary magnetic tape recording; but again, we do not know what forces cause the recording, and what 'picks it up'. (The late Tom Lethbridge thought that electrical fields are involved.) Telepathy is now so well authenticated that even the most sceptical psychical researchers would agree that it is now 'proven'; Upton Sinclair called it 'mental radio'; but again, we do not know anything about the transmitter, the receiver, or the 'ether' that carries the transmission.

But it is probably true to say that the basis of all 'occultism' in all ages has been a belief in some form of 'psychic ether' that can transmit thoughts, feelings, impulses and mental acts of will.

Magic is also based upon the notion that there exists a world of disembodied entities, or spirits, and that these can be persuaded to carry out certain tasks. Commonsense finds the idea unacceptable; but again, the study of modern witchcraft in Africa and Brazil suggests that it could be correct.

The earliest magic, then, involved trying to influence wild animals through drawings or clay models. Sorcerers then discovered that these methods would also work on human beings. Fertility rituals could be used for blasting crops as well as encouraging them. 'Black magic' came into being. Budge's book *Egyptian Magic* links together the use of 'shabti' figures — small wooden images placed in the tomb to perform services for the deceased in the afterworld — and other forms of ritual magic. In short — to state the obvious — magic sprang out of religion, and was always closely linked with it.

One of the earliest magical texts, *The Key of Solomon*, contains rituals for destroying enemies by cursing a waxen image, and for cursing food to make it cause illness. It is emphasised that these ceremonies must be pronounced *at the right time:* for example food is cursed when Mars or Saturn are in the ascendant. Ancient man was intuitively aware of the forces of the universe — of how the sun and moon affected the earth's magnetic field, and of how it was also influenced by the planets. The great stone circles were almost certainly calendars — or calculators — to enable the priests to perform their rituals at precisely the right moment, when the forces of the mind could combine with the forces of the earth. Again, this tradition can be found in all ritual magic.

An equally important part of ritual magic was — and is — the consecrating of talismans. Again, the assumption is that a state of mind can be 'recorded' upon natural objects. Stephen Skinner, a modern historian of magic, has written: 'Talismans are made to specific specifications of ritual purity and with specific designs for a particular type of energy. These work like storage batteries and, if properly consecrated, will go on performing their job for long after the

consecration, before they 'wind down'. It is the type of talisman that can be used extremely effectively by a person who merely knows the details of its construction, quite independent of any faith he may have in it.' He goes on: 'The main considerations for producing such talismans are (1) that the right kind of force (usually categorised by planet or element) is employed. (It is as much use using a talisman of Mars in an operation of love as trying to use a magnet to pick up wooden blocks.) (2) The talisman, like the battery, must be charged, by its cutting, casting and inscribing which are to be done in a specific way at a specific hour of each day, (3) the talisman, again like the battery, must be connected appropriately to the thing, event or person which it is designed to affect/alter or cause. If all this is done properly, the rawest non-psychic novice will get results.' According to Skinner, magic works because it is an exact science, designed to take advantage of certain energies of the solar system.

Skinner tells a story of a man who asked him to consecrate a talisman to cause a certain woman to leave her husband; he refused, but the man consecrated the talisman himself, following instructions from a book on magic. The following day the woman appeared on his doorstep, having left her husband. A few days later, she left him again to return to her husband — Skinner believes this was because the consecration of the talisman was performed without sufficient care. Another magical historian, Francis King, tells how the composer Peter Warlock ignored the advice that no one should use a method of consecrating talismans recommended by Abra-Melin the Mage without first having had contact with one's 'Holy Guardian Angel'. (King defines this as the 'deepest layer of consciousness, the ultimate ego'.) Warlock ignored this advice, and attempted to cause his estranged wife to return to him by lettering one of the Abra-Melin talismans on his arm. She returned to him but left him again, and he committed suicide shortly afterwards.

The real problem for anyone who studies the 'magical' works of such magicians as Cornelius Agrippa or Paracelsus — or a modern compilation like De Laurence's *Great Book of Magical Art* — is that they sound so preposterous. *The Key of Solomon* contains a ritual for preventing huntsmen from harming animals: a rod of green elder has to be hollowed out at both ends, and two small pieces of parchment made from the skin of a hare inserted in either end, one with a drawing of a fish's skeleton on it, the other with the word 'Abimegh'. It must be sealed with pitch, fumigated three times with incense on a Friday in February, and buried under an elder tree where the huntsman is expected to pass. Yet before dismissing this as a complete absurdity, consider the story of the stage magician and mind reader Wolf Messing, who fled from Poland to the Soviet Union during the second world war. To demonstrate his powers to Stalin, Messing offered to enter his country *dacha*

without a pass. In fact, he walked coolly into the grounds and past the guards, who stood aside respectfully to let him pass. He walked into Stalin's study, and explained that he had simply used a form of mental suggestion to make the guards think he was Beria, head of the secret police. He also demonstrated his powers by walking into a bank and handing the teller a note apparently asking for 100,000 roubles in cash. Without blinking, the bank clerk handed over the money; five minutes later, accompanied by two bank officials, Messing walked in and handed it back. The bank clerk had a heart attack when he realised that what Messing had handed him was, in fact, a sheet of blank paper. (Both stories can be found in *Psychic Discoveries Behind the Iron Curtain* by Schroeder and Ostrander.)

Messing apparently possessed a power that many 'psychics' and magicians have claimed: to influence other people's minds. (The playwright Strindberg was convinced he could make himself 'invisible' by suggestion.) This is clearly a form of 'magic'. And *if* such mental powers could be somehow imprinted upon physical objects, then presumably the magic of the *Key of Solomon* might also work.

A major change in the whole magical tradition occurred some time towards the end of the 13th century when a vast commentary on the first five books of Moses, the *Zohar*, began to be circulated. It seems to have been written — or edited — by a Spanish rabbi, Moses de Leon, but it is the general opinion of scholars that it reaches back at least fifteen centuries before that. It must be remembered that the basic tradition of magic *and* mysticism is that the material world is only the facade of a far more complex reality — that is, of a spiritual world. What the Kabbalah claims to describe is the structure of this spiritual world. Our material world is an emanation of God; but this is only one of ten. It is, in fact, the lowest. The diagram of the arrangement of these ten 'emanations' forms a pattern known as the 'tree of life'. The ten emanations, or Sephiroth, are joined by twenty two lines, known as paths. The concept has become much easier to grasp since Aldous Huxley's two two little books on mescalin popularised the idea that our 'inner worlds' are as vast as the world we live in. Add to that William Blake's notion that eternity opens from the centre of an atom, and we have the notion of a spiritual world in another dimension from the physical, which becomes accessible by a kind of descent into oneself.

The Kabbalah became the basis of the magical 'systems' of Cornelius Agrippa, Paracelsus, and such 20th century occultists as Aleister Crowley and Dion Fortune. In effect, the Kabbalah was adapted to the magical system of the gentile world by students like Ficino, Pico della Mirandola and Agrippa. Their 'magic' is also permeated with the idea of 'celestial influences' — the planets — and the 'correspondences' between these influences and terrestrial objects.

The cabbalistic 'Tree of Life'.

CHAPTER 13
Werewolves

In his classic study *Man into Wolf,* the Jungian psychologist Robert Eisler advances the view that man was once a peaceful vegetarian, but that his battles against wild animals gradually developed a blood-lust in him, which reappears among civilised men as sadism and lycanthropy — that is, the delusion of certain madmen that they can turn into wolves.

In 1521, a traveller in the Poligny district of France was attacked by a wolf; he defended himself so vigorously that he wounded it. Following the trail of blood, he found his way to a hut; inside, to his astonishment, there was a woman who was bathing the wounds of a naked man. The man, Michel Verdung, was arrested, and implicated two more men, Pierre Bourgot and Philibert Mentot. Bourgot confessed that he was a servant of the devil. In 1502, his flocks had been scattered by a storm, and he met three black horsemen, one of whom, named Moyset, offered to help him find his sheep if he would agree to serve him. Pierre agreed, and quickly recovered all his sheep. The man came to claim his reward, and Pierre had to swear fealty to the Devil and kiss the man's left hand, which was black and cold as ice. When, two years later, Pierre seemed inclined to drift back to church, another servant of the devil, Michel Verdung, was ordered to make him live up to his bargain. Pierre described how he had attended a Sabbat with Verdung, at which he had stripped and been rubbed all over with ointment; he then changed into a wolf. Later, he was rubbed with another ointment, and changed back. Philibert Mentot was also present. Under torture, Pierre Bourgot admitted eating two children — both girls — and to mating with female wolves. The other two also admitted to this practice and said it gave them as much pleasure as mating with their wives. All three were burned.

In 1573, there were a number of attacks on young children in Dôle, Franche-Comté. On November 9 of that year, peasants heard a child screaming and found her being attacked by a large wolf, which fled on their approach. A few days later, when a small boy was missing, a peasant named Gilles Garnier was arrested; he was a recluse who lived in a remote hut near Armanges with his wife. Garnier confessed to all the attacks on children. In August, he had attacked and killed a twelve year old boy in a pear orchard. About to eat him, he was forced to flee by the approach of some men. On this occasion, he was in his own shape. But in October he had changed into a wolf, and killed and ate a ten year old girl. He enjoyed her flesh so much that he took some home for his wife. In November he attacked another girl, but was forced to flee when people approached. And on November 15, just before his arrest, he had killed a ten year old boy — again in his animal shape — and eaten one of his legs. Garnier was burned alive in January 1574.

In 1598, a sixteen year old boy named Benoit Bidel of Naizan, in the Jura, was found dying at the foot of a tree from a stab wound. He claimed that he had been up a tree picking fruit, leaving his sister below, when the girl was attacked by a wolf. Benoit climbed down to help her, flourishing his knife. He claimed that the wolf had human hands instead of forepaws, and that it snatched his knife and stabbed him. Benoit then died. Peasants searching the area found a semi-imbecile girl named Perrenette Gandillon, whom they took to be the werewolf, and killed her.

Peasants recalled that Perrenette's brother Pierre had a strangely unpleasant appearance, as if scarred with scratches. He was also arrested, together with his sister Antoinette and his son George. All three confessed to attending Sabbats and turning themselves into wolves with 'salve' or ointment Judge Henri Boguet, author of a famous *Discourse on Sorcerers,* visited the three self-confessed werewolves in jail, and said they ran around on all fours. When he asked them to turn themselves into wolves, they replied that this was impossible, since they had no ointment or salve.

It is interesting to note that Pierre Gandillon had fallen into a trance on Maundy Thursday, and when he recovered, claimed that his spirit had attended a Sabbat of werewolves. It raises the question of whether some self-confessed werewolves may have been in a state of trance or 'astral projection', like the porpoise-caller described by Grimble (see Introduction). Again, there are circumstantial confes-

sions by witches in which they describe flying through the air after anointing themselves with a 'flying ointment', and the occult-historian Stephen Skinner has raised the question of whether the ointment itself may have had certain hallucinatory properties; many hallucinatory drugs — of the same type as the *peyotl* cactus — can be found in common flowers in the hedgerow.

In the same year — 1598 — a beggar named Jacques Roulet was charged with being a werewolf. A group of armed men had come upon the mutilated body of a boy and thought they saw two wolves running away. They gave chase and cornered a 'wolf' — only to find that it was a filthily clad man, who had blood on his face and beard. Tried at Angers, Roulet admitted to being a *loup garou* and attacking children. Asked if his hands became paws, he answered yes; but admitted that he was not sure whether his head became a wolf's head. The questions reveal that the court was sceptical; and, in fact, Roulet escaped with two years in an asylum.

Another case in which a court declined to believe that 'shape-shifting' was possible was that of Jean Grenier, reported by Pierre de Lancre, magistrate and well-known writer on witchcraft and sorcery. In 1603, in the department of Les Landes, an odd-looking youth got into conversation with some girls tending sheep, and announced that he was a werewolf and had eaten girls. He had black hair and prominent teeth, and (as later evidence showed) was mentally defective. But since a number of children had been killed in the area, and three girls claimed to have been attacked by him, Grenier was arrested. He implicated his father and a neighbour, M. del Thillaire, who were also arrested and tortured. His father pointed out that his son was widely known to be an idiot, and that he claimed to have slept with every woman for miles around. What seems certain is that Jean was sexually overdeveloped, and spent much of his time lying in the undergrowth near a pool where girls went to bathe. He claimed to have attacked two naked girls and killed one of them, dragging her off and eating her over two days (which is clearly impossible). Jean claimed that M. del Thillaire had taken him into the forest when he was ten and introduced him to a 'black man', who 'signed' him with his nail and gave him a wolf skin and a salve to turn himself into a wolf.

The Parlement of Bordeaux reviewed the case, sent two doctors to look at Grenier, and accepted their report that Jean was an imbecile who suffered from a mental malady known as lycanthropy — that is, he suffered from the delusion that he changed into a wolf. And so Jean was condemned to imprisonment in a local monastery, and the two men were released. De Lancre went to see Jean two years later, and describes him as of small stature, very shy — he would not look anyone in the face — and with black teeth and nails.

72

Although he still maintained he had been a werewolf and eaten children, he otherwise seemed to be unable to understand the simplest questions. He died in 1610, 'as a good Christian', at the age of twenty. Grenier was undoubtedly lucky; Bordeaux was one of the major centres of witch persecution at this period.

The most extreme sentence passed on a 'werewolf' was that delivered in the case of Peter Stubbe or Stumpf in 1589. There had been a large number of wolf attacks in the Cologne area of Germany, and matters came to a head when a wolf attacked a group of children playing in the meadows and tried to tear out the throat of one child; fortunately, she wore a high, stiff collar. There were cattle nearby with young calves, and they attacked the wolf, which ran away. Men and dogs began to organise into hunts, and one day, a group of hunters came close to capturing the wolf. At this point, they saw a man with a staff walking towards the city, and decided that — since the wolf had vanished — he must be a werewolf. This was Peter Stubbe. He was arrested and tortured, and had soon confessed to an amazing series of attacks. To begin with, Stubbe confessed to incest with his daughter — with whom he had a child — and his sister; he was living with a woman called Katherine Trompin. The pamphlet 'translated out of the high Dutch' and printed in London in June 1590, goes on to assert that the Devil now sent Stubbe a beautiful succubus with whom he lived for seven years. At some point, the Devil gave Stubbe a belt with which he could transform himself into a wolf and — according to the pamphlet — he killed and ate his own son in this guise. Over a period of twenty five years he had 'destroyed and spoiled an unknown number of men, women and children, sheep, lambs, and goats and other cattle..'

The magistrates searched for the magic belt in the valley where Stubbe claimed to have hidden it, but were unable to find it; they decided the Devil had taken it back.

Stubbe seems to have implicated his daughter and mistress in his confession, and they were also tried. They were sentenced to be burned, but Stubbe was sentenced to be broken on a wheel, his flesh pulled off with red hot pincers, and then decapitated. The sentences were carried out on October 31, 1589. The case aroused widespread interest all over Europe, and many commentaries on it exists. But it is difficult not to suspect that Stubbe was merely an unlucky man who happened to be walking past when the wolf disappeared.

CHAPTER 14

Dame Alice Kyteler

Among all the appalling stories of persecution and torture in the history of witchcraft, it is pleasant to read of the case of a woman who gave as good as she got, and escaped with her life. But it seems highly likely that Dame Alice *was* guilty — if not of witchcraft, then of straightforward poisoning.

Dame Alice Kyteler, the first Irish witch, lived in Kilkenny in the early years of the fourteenth century — that is, after the burning of the Cathars, but before witchcraft became a crime in itself.

Dame Alice had been married four times: to William Outlawe, a wealthy banker, who died before 1302, to Adam le Blond, who died about 1311 and to Richard de Valle. Her fourth husband, who was alive but ailing when Dame Alice was charged with sorcery, was Sir John le Poer.

In 1324, Sir John's children observed that he was wasting away, his hair coming out in handfuls, and wondered if he was being killed by sorcery. Sir John demanded the key of his wife's room and finally took them from her forcibly; in the room, he found locked boxes and chests, which proved to contain powders and unguents. Sir John concluded that she was engaging in sorcery. He sent the chests and boxes to the Bishop of Ossory, Richard de Landrede, who had trained in France and knew all about witches and witchcraft. The bishop ordered an investigation, as a result of which he charged Dame Alice and eleven

accomplices with heresy, sacrificing to demons, (the chief of whom was called Robin Artison, or Robin son of Art), performing 'black masses', and killing her previous husbands by sorcery. The accused included her son, William Outlawe, and her maid Petronilla.

In Ireland then, as now, the 'gentry' were much respected, and the Bishop found it hard to get Dame Alice arrested by officers of the law. He tried excommunicating her, and Dame Alice retaliated by getting him arrested and lodged in Kilkenny jail. He was kept there for seventeen days, then released. He meanwhile placed the whole diocese under interdict and censure, but the Lord Justice, Sir Arnold le Poer (probably a relative of Dame Alice's husband) appealed to Dublin, charging an illegal ban, and the Bishop had to lift it. Next time the Lord Justice held court, the Bishop turned up carrying the sacrament, and a vigorous war of words ensued, which ended with the Bishop being thrown out. He came a second time to demand the arrest of Dame Alice and her son; again he was thrown out.

Dame Alice, still determined, had the Bishop summoned to Dublin to answer for having excommunicated her when she was as yet unconvicted of sorcery. The court was against the Bishop; but he seems to have been a singularly stubborn man, and persisted; the court finally agreed that Dame Alice and the Lord Justice were in the wrong in refusing to submit to the law. Sir Arnold had to apologise, and to agree to do his duty. Dame Alice decided to flee to England. Her son, William Outlawe, was arrested, and spent nine weeks in jail. He decided to confess to all the charges — probably having been assured that he would be let off with a penance. So it was; he was made to re-roof the Cathedral at his own expense, and make a pilgrimage to the shrine of St Thomas at Canterbury. The other eight people charged also decided that it would be simplest to confess and to lay all the blame on Dame Alice. The maid Petronilla, after being flogged six times, confessed to all kinds of wickedness, including having sex with Robin Artison, and working a spell against her own husband. She was sentenced to death and burned. The others were sentenced to be whipped in the market place and through the streets of Kilkenny. Dame Alice herself was sentenced *in absentia*, and her lands were presumably forfeited — which some writers on the case suspect was the basic motive behind the accusations of heresy. If this *was* the case, then it must have been a satisfaction to Dame Alice — safe in England — to hear that Ledrede himself was subsequently accused of heresy, made his way to Avignon to see the Pope, and had all his lands seized by the Crown in the meantime. He was acquitted, only be accused again ten years later and again deprived of his lands and possessions. No doubt Dame Alice was making wax images of him and sticking pins in them.

CHAPTER 15

The Chelmsford Witch Trials

In spite of the *Malleus Maleficarum* and the Bull of Innocent VIII, the witchcraft fever took a long time to spread across Europe; in the first half of the 16th century, there were only occasional cases — like the werewolves of Poligny (see chapter on Werewolves) or the trial of the unfortunate Madame Desle la Mansenée at Luxeuil in 1529, when the Inquisition seems to have based its case on the hearsay evidence of neighbours. Martin Luther and John Calvin had more to do with the rise of the witchcraft fever than the various Popes who issued bulls against it. The Church once again felt itself to be seriously challenged — as in the 13th century, by the Cathars. In France in 1557, forty witches were burned at Toulouse — centre of the Catharist heresy. Witchcraft came to England with the witchcraft bill passed under Queen Elizabeth in 1563. At Chelmsford in 1566, three women were charged with different acts of witchcraft, the only connection being that they all came from the same village, Hatfield Peverell. In the case of one of these women, Elizabeth Francis, the evidence suggests that she was, indeed, a witch. She was accused of bewitching a child and making it ill, and seems to have admitted openly that she had learned witchcraft from her grandmother at the age of twelve, and that she had a 'familiar', a cat called Sathan, which bewitched people for her. She told how she had wanted to marry a man named William Byles, and how her cat had advised her to

seduce him, which she did; however he still declined to marry her, so she allowed the cat to kill him by witchcraft. She claimed that the cat had helped her abort Byles's child, and that had later advised her to sleep with a yeoman named Christopher Francis and get herself pregnant; Francis married her. Oddly enough, Elizabeth Francis was sentenced to only one year in prison.

Another woman charged with her — Agnes Waterhouse — was less lucky, she confessed to attempting to bewitch a neighbour named William Fynee to death and to attempting to bewitch another neighbour without success. (She had been given the cat Sathan by Elizabeth Francis.) Mother Waterhouse (as she was known) was hanged — the first woman in England to be hanged for witchcraft. Her daughter Joan, was found not guilty of bewitching a girl. But Elizabeth Francis was to appear before the same court on two future occasions, charged with witchcraft; on the second she received another year in jail, and on the third, was hanged.

In 1582 there was another famous witch trial at Chelmsford — selected by the sceptic Reginald Scot, author of *The Discovery of Witchcraft* — as a typical example of the witchcraft delusion; however, Scot gets his figures wrong — he says there were seventeen or eighteen women executed, whereas there were only two.

The case began with a quarrel between an old woman named Ursula Kempe, a nurse and midwife, and a woman named Grace Thorlowe. Mrs Thorlowe refused to hire Ursula Kempe to nurse her new born daughter, and when the child fell out of her cot and broke her neck, Grace suspected Ursula of *maleficia* (black witchcraft). Some time after, Grace refused to pay Ursula for her help in alleviating her arthritis on the grounds that it had been ineffective — the pains had come back. Grace complained to a county sessions judge for whom she worked, and Ursula Kempe was arrested and charged with witchcraft. She admitted to some 'white witchcraft' — simple healing — and was finally induced to confess to *maleficia* when the Judge, Bryan Darcy, hinted at clemency if she confessed and execution if she didn't. Thereupon Ursula Kempe confessed to many acts of witchcraft, such as destroying cattle and bewitching a woman to death; she also confessed to causing the cradle of the dead child to overturn, and to bewitching the child of another woman who had accompanied Grace to complain to the magistrate. She went on to accuse a dozen other people of being involved in witchcraft with her. Some confessed, some insisted they were not guilty. Children were brought into court to describe their mother's 'imps' or familiars. 'The said Ursula Kemple had four spyrites, viz. Tetty a hee like a gray cat, Jacke a hee like a black cat, Pygin a shee like a black toad, and Tyffin a she like a white lambe..'

The court seems to have shown remarkably good sense, discharging eleven of the accused, and hanging only two, including Ursula — who had been promised clemency.

The trial has been strongly condemned by many who have written about it — on legal grounds — and it is true that the court accepted evidence that we would regard as completely inadmissible. Yet it is important to try to put ourselves in the minds of the people involved. A baby had died of a broken neck after falling out of its crib, and after the mother had quarrelled with a woman who seemed to have genuine powers as a witch (i.e. she had temporarily cured Grace's athritis). When Grace and a friend went to complain to the magistrate, the friend's child also became ill with strange swellings of the privy and hind parts, and also died. It must have looked fairly obvious to everyone involved that Ursula Kempe was 'getting away with murder'.

These events might be compared with an item that appeared in the London *Daily Mail* on March 6, 1981, describing how all four daughters of Donald Shreeves, of Pexoria, Illinois, had died by violence at different times: the first in a car crash in 1972, the second when she happened to look out of her front door to investigate firing noises, and she was shot through the head by a gangster who had just killed her next door neighbour, the third when she went to Chicago to investigate her sister's murder — she was found dead in a lift with an overdose of drugs — and the fourth shot by her husband. Donald Shreeves is quoted as saying: 'What the hell is wrong with us? Did we drink out of the wrong side of the cup, or what?' Three centuries ago, it would have struck him as a perfectly logical hypothesis that someone had 'put a hex' on him. And it may be regarded as one possibility, if we are willing to admit the possibility of *maleficia* — as do James H. Neal, author of *Ju-Ju in My Life* and Father Dupreyat, author of *Mitsinari* (both described in the Introduction) and many others who have had experience of African witchcraft.

On the available evidence, it seems not at all improbable that a great deal of simple witchcraft went on in the Chelmsford area during the reign of Queen Elizabeth I, and that some of the witches genuinely tried to use their powers for *maleficia*. Possibly they succeeded. So while most of us will be inclined to dismiss all the evidence about familiars and demons as hysteria, it is necessary to admit that this may not have been entirely a case of smoke without fire.

There were two more major witch trials at Chelmsford, one in 1589, when ten people were charged with *maleficia* and four were hanged, and the fourth — the most notorious witch trial of the century, in 1645 (see Matthew Hopkins). In the third trial, the details were so similar to those in the others — toads, cats, black imps, and so on — that there would be no point in going into further detail. But it could be significant that three of the 'witches' all made final confessions on the scaffold, when they might have been expected to protest their innocence.

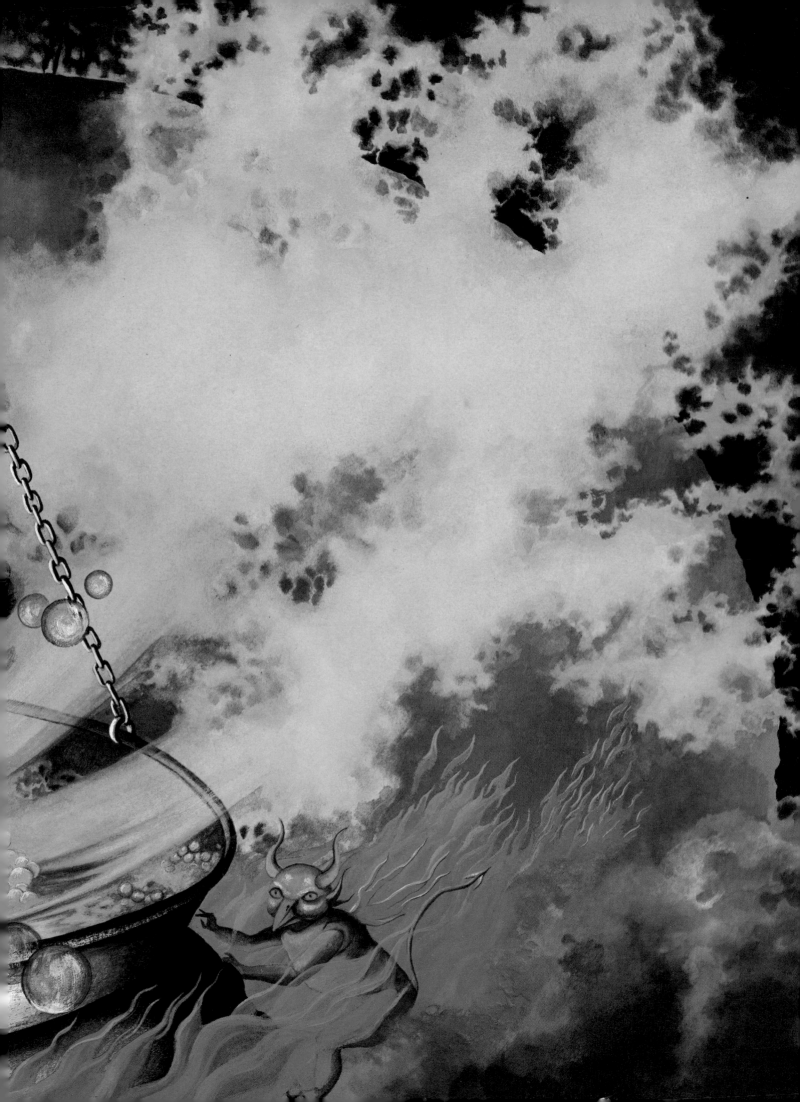

CHAPTER 16
Witchcraft in Germany

In Germany, thousands of people had been executed for witchcraft by the beginning of the seventeenth century, most of them tortured, many burned alive; thousands more would die before the persecutions came to a halt.

In Treves, five women were burned as witches in 1572, but this was only a prelude to the trials that began in 1582. By then, the harvest had been poor for several years, and witches were blamed. (Such troubles often seem to cause witch persecutions; a hundred years later, Massachusetts was having all kinds of political problems when the Salem 'witch scare' helped to release the sense of oppression and helplessness.) Between 1587 and 1594, 306 persons were accused of being witches, and they involved another six thousand people in their confessions as accomplices. In his *History of Treves* Johan Linden, canon of the cathedral, notes: 'Scarcely any of those who were accused escaped punishment'. Dietrich Flade, Vice-Governor of Treves and Rector of the university, objected that many of the trials were illegal, and was himself accused as a witch and burned.

Franz Buirmann was a German equivalent of the English 'witch-finder' Matthew Hopkins; but there were many like him, and his career has survived only because Hermann Löher, a humanitarian court official who was forced to flee to Holland, wrote about his personal knowledge of Buirmann in a book published many years later. Löher lived at

Right A suspect being subjected to the strappado, a device for dislocating the joints.

Rheinbach, near Bonn, a quiet village that had little crime. Buirmann, described as a 'shrewd man of low birth', had been appointed itinerant judge and witch-hunter by the Archbishop of Cologne; he was able to claim the property of those he condemned as witches, and as a consequence, became affluent. In 1631 and 1636 he paid two visits to Rheinbach and two nearby villages, and burned 150 people out of 300 households. In further persecutions at Siegburg later the same year, Buirmann even had the executioner burned as a witch.

The German witch persecutions occurred mainly in towns that remained Catholic (like Treves). Other such areas were Strasbourg, Breslau, Fulda, Würzburg and Bamberg. Würzburg and Bamberg were ruled by cousins, one of whom burned 900 people, the other 600. In Bamberg, the witch burning began around 1609, under Bishop von Aschhausen, who in thirteen years burned 300 witches. In another series of trials between 1626 and 1630, 400 people were burned. When the Vice-Chancellor tried stopping the trials, he was accused as a witch and executed with his wife and daughter. (The Prince-Archbishop ignored an order from the Emperor ordering their release.) But the Bamberg trials stopped as abruptly as they had started, in 1630, partly because of the invasion of Leipzig by the Swedish King Gustavus, which gave the instigators of the trials other things to think about, partly because of the continued opposition of the Emperor.

In Würzburg in 1629, the Chancellor described in a letter how he had seen many children executed for intercourse with the devil — their ages ranging from three to fifteen. He adds that it is 'beyond doubt that in a place called the Fraw Rengberg the Devil in person with 8,000 of his followers held an assembly and celebrated a black mass'. In 1629 there were twenty nine executions totalling 157 persons, many of them children. The Prince-Bishop even had his sole heir, a youth, beheaded as a witch. After this execution, the Prince-Bishop seems to have experienced a change of heart, and instituted commemorative services for the victims. Here, as in Bamberg, the Inquisitors and witch-finders were Jesuits. Prince-Bishop Philip Adolf, the man responsible for all these deaths, is described by one historian as 'otherwise noble and pious'.

Yet there were .waves of revulsion and resistance to all the torture and murder. In 1663, a magistrate and 'witch-finder' named Geiss, who had been torturing and burning the citizens of Lindheim for two years, turned his attention to a wealthy miller named Johann Schüler. (Here, as in so many other cases, the basic motive was undoubtedly financial.) Schuler's wife had borne a stillborn child the previous year, and Geiss forced the midwife to 'confess' that they had murdered the child and used the body for witchcraft. The child's body was exhumed and found to be intact (the

midwife alleged it had been cut up), and the midwife and six people she had implicated were burned. Not long after, Geiss persuaded another suspected witch — through torture — to implicate Frau Schüler, who was arrested; an old scar was declared to be a 'devil's mark'. Schüler hastened to Würzburg to try to persuade the Dean of the Cathedral to help, but in his absence, Frau Schüler was tortured into confession. On his return, Schüler was thrown into the 'witch's tower' and then tortured into confessing. However, as soon as the torture stopped, he recanted. He was tortured again; again he confessed and recanted. Geiss was preparing to torture him a third time when angry townspeople rioted, and Schüler and other suspected witches managed to escape. They succeeded in getting to Speyer, the seat of the Supreme Court, where the sight of their tortured and scarred bodies — particularly the women — aroused indignation. But in Schüler's absence, and in spite of popular anger, Geiss burnt Frau Schüler alive. The townspeople rose up in force, and Geiss and his men had to flee. The Dean of Würzburg suggested to Baron Oynhausen — responsible for Geiss's appointment — that he ought to assuage the popular fury by censuring Geiss, and Oynhausen dismissed him, to Geiss's indignation — he insisted that he had only been doing his duty.

The Protestant states executed less witches, and ceased the witchcraft persecutions, earlier than Catholic states; in Prussia, King Frederick William put a stop to witch trials in 1714. The last execution for witchcraft in Germany took place in 1775.

Why were the witch trials so widespread in Germany — more than in any other country? Rossell Hope Robbins comments; 'Germany was the land of torture.....' and cites a case in Tettwang, near Constance, in 1608, when a father died in prison from torture, his wife was hoisted in the strappado eleven times (a device for dislocating the shoulders), and their 29 year old daughter was also hoisted eleven times with a fifty pound weight attached to her legs. The torturer allowed her to recover for ten weeks before subjecting her to more torture — not out of mercy, but because he was afraid she would die under it.

The case of Buirmann and Geiss makes it obvious that many of the 'witch-finders' were sexual sadists, for whom the persecutions were an opportunity to give free rein to their impulses. (Criminologists have noted that Germany has a higher percentage of mass murders and sadistic murders than any other country — although in the past few decades America is beginning to catch up.) The rise of Protestantism in Germany also seems to explain a great deal (although some cities that persecuted witches — like Leipzig — were Protestant) as the Catholic Church struggled to regain its authority through a reign of terror.

CHAPTER 17

Gilles de Rais

Like the Marquis de Sade, Gilles de Rais remains one of those symbolic figures whose significance continues to trouble us even after we have dismissed him as a self-indulgent sadist.

Born in 1404, Gilles became the richest nobleman in Europe but he was also spoilt, imperious and destructive. He was obsessed with the excesses of the Romans Tiberius and Caligula and strove to emulate their lifestyles, not only copying them in extravagance but also in sexual deviance and debauchery with a preference for young children, enlisting the help of his cousins and others to procure and later kill the children involved. When Gilles was 25, he met Joan of Arc and became fascinated with her boyish figure and, in effect, fell in love with her. But after fighting bravely by her side he stood by and watched her condemned to be burnt as a witch. In *The Witch Cult in Western Europe*, Margaret Murray states her conviction that both Gilles and Joan of Arc were members of the 'Dianic Cult', and this is why he made no attempt to rescue the maid — she was a sacrifice, a martyr for the Old Religion. After her death, Gilles returned to his estates and began putting into practice his dreams of being one of the Caesars.

His financial excess finally began to drain even his great resources and at some point Gilles decided he ought to try repairing his fortunes by alchemy — turning base metals into gold. He seems to have read a book on alchemy as early as

1426. About ten years later, when Giles's fortunes were plunging, he asked one of his employees, a priest named Blanchet, to find him a magician — although it seems that his cousin de Sillé had already introduced him to a number of practitioners of the black arts. Few results were obtained — although one magician named Fontenelle succeeded in invoking twenty crowns, and claimed that he had invoked a demon named Barron.

Magicians in those days were convinced that magical acts were performed through the agency of the Devil and his legions; so there can be no doubt that Gilles believed he was endangering his soul — playing a more dangerous game than any so far. And he was terrified of the consequences. At the castle of Tiffauges, Gilles and his cousin de Sillé locked themselves in a basement with a magician to perform magic; the magician warned him solemnly not to make the sign of the cross, or he would be in great danger. At a certain point, Gilles and his cousin fled from the room, and heard thumping noises behind them. Looking into the room, they found that the magician had apparently been badly beaten 'so hurt that he could hardly stand up'; they were afraid that he would die, but he recovered. So Gilles was convinced he was dealing with the powers of hell — although he later insisted that he had resolutely refused to sell his soul to the Devil. When one magician drowned on his way to the castle, and another died soon after he arrived, Gilles took these to be signs and warnings. Yet he now needed money so badly that there seemed no way to retreat. Occasionally, he toyed with the idea of making a pilgrimage to Jerusalem and confessing all his sins; but the attraction of his favourite sexual indulgences was too strong.

The priest Blanchet was sent to Italy in 1439 in search of more magicians; he found a 'clerk in minor orders' called François Prelati, who claimed to be an alchemist. Prelati seems to have been a young man, about twenty three, who set determinedly about trying to invoke the Devil, as well as the demon Barron. He himself received a violent beating from the demons on one occasion — unless, as seems probable, the episode was staged to convince Gilles that the experiments were not entirely a fraud.

Gilles became deeply depressed. He now committed the act that was to cause his downfall. He had sold a castle called Malemort to a man called Geoffroy de Ferron, treasurer to Jean V, Duke of Brittany. Gilles decided to repossess it by force; while Geoffrey was absent, the keys were held by his brother, a priest, and Gilles marched into his church, had him beaten, and thrown in a dungeon. It was the opportunity the Duke had been waiting for. For some time, he and the Bishop of Nantes had been wondering how they could cause Gilles's downfall and seize his lands. Now, by attacking a member of the Church — and of the Duke's household — he had left himself wide open. The Duke imposed a huge

fine, which Gilles could not pay, and started an investigation into the disappearance of children.

Even now Gilles continued to assault and kill children. His last murder was committed in August 1440, he had a page-boy suit made for a boy who entered his service, but the child was quickly assaulted and killed. The corpse was burnt.

In September 1440, Gilles was arrested, and taken to Nantes. His trial began on the 13 of October, 1440. The indictment was forty nine paragraphs long, one of which declared that for fourteen years 'possessed by the Evil One', he had 'took, killed and cut the throats of many children, boys and girls'. The indictment insisted that Gilles's crimes had begun in 1426; Gilles himself insisted it was 1433, and at this point he had no reason to lie.

At first, Gilles answered all charges with arrogance and defiance. But after being subjected to strong moral pressure and threat of excommunication, he caved in and recognised the competence of the court. The Duke and Bishop must have heaved sigh of relief; if Gilles had persisted in refusing to co-operate, he would almost certainly have escaped.

The prosecutor representing the secular authorities tried hard to make Gilles say that his crimes were inspired by the Devil; but Gilles insisted — truthfully — that 'he did them in accordance with his own imagination'. Nevertheless, he seemed to be willing to confess everything and to throw himself on the mercy of the court. He shed tears and begged the forgiveness of the parents of the children he had killed — the charge mentioned a hundred and forty, but the true number is probably more than twice that — and parents in court wept and forgave him. There can be no doubt that they were awed by the prospect of his eternal damnation. The Bishop covered over the crucifix and Gilles confessed to one murder after another.

Gilles was sentenced to death — to be hanged first, then burned. His two servants Henriet and Poitou were sentenced to die with him. Prelati was sentenced to life imprisonment — in fact, he escaped, only to be hanged for further crimes. Another procurer of children, a woman named Perrine Martin, hanged herself in her cell. Gilles's two cousins, who committed so many of the murders, seem to have escaped unpunished. Gilles was thirty six when he died; his lands were seized by the Duke and the Bishop.

Some writers on the case have suggested that Gilles was 'framed' — that he never murdered anyone. That view is inadmissible. His murders were quite unconnected with his attempts to repair his fortune by means of the black arts; there is no evidence that he used children as human sacrifices to the Devil — although he let Prelati make magical use of parts of the dismembered corpses. He was sentenced for heresy, and the Church could have burned him for heresy without charging him with the murders.

CHAPTER 18
Mother Shipton

The famous 'witch' and prophetess Mother Shipton may be a figure of legend; but there is some evidence for her real existence. A book of her prophecies published in 1797 by 'S. Baker' gives the following biographical details: she was born in Yorkshire near Knaresborough in the reign of Henry VII, and baptised by the Abbot of Beverley as Ursula Sonthiel. 'Her stature was larger than common, her body crooked, her face frightful; but her understanding extraordinary...' But there seems to be some doubt about her birth some attributing it to 1448, others to 1488; since one of her most famous prophecies concerns the arrest of Cardinal Wolsey (1530) the latter seems more likely.

She is described as a 'very pious person', married to a carpenter named Toby Shipton. They lived in the village of Skipton four miles north of York.

Like Nostradamus, she seems to have made many of her prophesies in rhyme. The most famous reads:

'Carriages without horses shall go
And accidents fill the world with woe.
Around the earth thought shall fly
In the twinkling of an eye.
The world upside down shall be
And gold found at the root of a tree.
Through hills man shall ride

And no horse be at his side.
Under water men shall walk
Shall ride, shall sleep, shall talk.
In the air men shall be seen
In white, in black, in green.
Iron in the water shall float,
As easily as a wooden boat.
Gold shall be found and shown
In a land that's now not known.
Fire and water shall wonders do,
England shall at last admit a foe.
The world to an end shall come
In eighteen hundred and eighty one.'

In view of her excellent guesses in predicting motor cars, aeroplanes, submarines, iron ships and gold in California (or the Yukon or South Africa), it seems a pity that she should spoil it by naming a date for the end of the world.

The most famous story of her concerns Cardinal Wolsey. When she heard that the Cardinal intended to come and live in York, Mother Shipton went on record as saying he would never reach that city. The Cardinal sent three lords of his retinue to check on her. She was living at the time in a village called Dring Houses, to the west of York. The story states that although they were incognito she knew who they

were. When asked if she had said that the Cardinal would never see York, she replied that he would see it, but never reach it. One of them remarked: 'When he gets to York he will surely burn you as a witch', whereupon Mother Shipton tossed her hankerchief in the fire and said: 'If this burns, so shall I'. The hankerchief remained unscorched. One of the Lords, Thomas Cromwell, asked her about his own future, and she replied that 'the time will come when you shall be as low as I am'. Cromwell was, of course, beheaded.

Her prophecy about Wolsey proved correct. He arrived at Cawood, eight miles from York, and viewed the city from the top of the castle tower. Before descending the stairs, he received a message saying the king wished to see him immediately. He turned back towards London but became ill on the road, and died at Leicester.

The astrologer William Lilly published several of Mother Shipton's prophecies in 1645. Of twenty prophecies he mentions sixteen as having been fulfilled, and singles out as unfulfilled a prophecy about mariners sailing up the Thames and the master weeping for what was once a goodly city and now there is scarce left any house that can let us have drinke for our money . S. Baker, in his edition, points out that this *was* fulfilled twenty one years after Lilly's edition, when the city was burnt by the Great Fire.

CHAPTER 19

Isobel Gowdie

The case of Isobel Gowdie is baffling because the confession was made freely, without any form of compulsion. Margaret Murray believes this is because Isobel was, in fact, a member of a fertility cult in which a man dressed up as the Devil for their earth-rituals. Rossell Hope Robbins takes the view that she was simply insane. Montague Summers, naturally, believes every word she confessed. None of these explanations seems to cover the facts.

In some respects the confessions of Isobel Gowdie and the Auldearne witches are amongst the most detailed in the history of such trials. But certain essential details are missing, such as Isobel Gowdie's age, and the sentence passed on her and her fellow witches.

Isobel Gowdie was an attractive, red-headed girl who married a farmer of Lochloy, near Auldearne in Morayshire. She was childless and her husband is said to have been a stupid and boorish man. In April 1662, she startled and shocked the elders of the local kirk when she announced that she had been a practising witch for the past fifteen years, had attended Sabbats, had sexual intercourse with the Devil and even killed people by witchcraft. She was tried at Auldearne, near Inverness, in the summer of 1662, together with others she had mentioned in her confession. Astonishingly enough, some of these confirmed what she said in detail.

According to Isobel — who made four confessions

between April and her trial — she encountered the Devil, a man dressed in grey, when she was travelling between two farms, and she seems to have promised herself to him and agreed to meet him at the church in Auldearne. She did so, and the Devil stood in the pulpit with a black book in his hand, and made her renounce Jesus. A woman called Margaret Brodie held her while the Devil sucked blood from her shoulder, making a Devil's mark, and baptised her. She described the Devil as a big, black, hairy man, who came to her a few days later and copulated with her. He would copulate freely with all the female witches, who thoroughly enjoyed it. (Another of the accused, Janet Breadhead, described how the women sat on either side of the Devil at a meeting, and next, the Devil copulated with all of them — which, unless he was phenomenally potent, seems to dispose of Margaret Murray's belief that he was a man dressed in a goat skin.) Sometimes the Devil changed himself to an animal — such as a deer or bull — before he copulated. It was Isobel who first used the word 'coven' of a group of witches, and declared that the number was thirteen. She said that each member had a spirit to wait upon her, (or him — there seem to have been male members). They had a Grand Meeting four times a year.

The confessions become wilder and stranger. She flew to Sabbats on a little horse. The witches could change themselves into any shape they wished, such as a cat, a hare, a crow. They would blast people's harvests and kill their children — Janet Breadhead says they made clay images of children, which were continually watered and baked until the child died; in this way, she says, they killed two children of the local laird, who was himself later bewitched to death. Isobel Gowdie says she killed several people using arrows given to her by the Devil. She also described a visit to fairyland, when the Downie Hill opened, and they were all generously fed by the Queen of the Faery, who was clothed in white linen. Afterwards they went shooting with the Devil; Isobel shot a woman, and the others brought down a ploughman.

It is a pity that no trial records have been found, so we have no idea of whether the witches were all sentenced to be burned — most commentators feel reasonably certain that they were, and, given the verdicts in similar trials at the time, this seems highly likely.

The mystery remains. The whole thing could not have been Isobel's fantasy, or the others would not have confirmed what she said (no mention of torture is made). Margaret Murray's 'Old Religion' theory has to be stretched too far to cover so many weird and wonderful events — in many of her accounts of witchcraft trials, she deliberately leaves out some of the more preposterous details, which would conflict with her view that the Devil was simply Grand Master of the coven and a priest of the Old Religion.

In *The Occult* I have suggested that the whole thing must be regarded as a figment of Isobel's imagination, stimulated by morbid sexual imaginings and wishful thinking. And certainly, Freud would have no difficulty in recognising sexual hysteria as the psychological driving force behind most of the confessions. But this still fails to explain why the others confirmed Isobel's confession.

The likeliest possibility is that a great deal of witch-craft — possibly a survival of old fertility rituals — *did* exist in that area, and may have been the excuse for sexual orgies. Isolated country areas seem to breed sexual irregularities — as a glance at newspaper records of their local assizes will verify. Once Isobel and the others had become involved in such matters, they would undoubtedly feel convinced that they had given themselves to Satan and were damned. Possibly there were even ceremonies to raise spirits — the equivalent of modern seances — and the results of such seances are unpredictable. Possibly Isobel was telling what she believed to be the truth when she said the Devil came to her in bed and copulated with her beside her sleeping husband. All that seems clear is that she believed in her confession, and that there was enough truth in it for others to confirm it. This makes it difficult to dismiss all such tales of Sabbats as illusions.

CHAPTER 20
Witches' Salve

Professor Erich-Will Peuckert of Göttingen University, is convinced that he has discovered the secret of the 'witches salve' that enabled them to fly to Sabbats on broomsticks. The journalist John Dunning has described Peuckert's researches into ancient books on magic and alchemy, and his consequent conviction that many of the magical recipes actually work. Peuckert tried the formula for training a savage dog — feeding it a piece of bread that the trainer has kept under his armpit for a day. Peuckert claims that this works because the bread absorbs the body-scent of the trainer, and that when the dog eats the bread, it becomes psychologically predisposed to that person — it has accepted him as if he were a fellow dog.

Peuckert then set out to test similar magical recipes for love potions. Extracts of skin oils and saliva were obtained from male students, purified chemically and injected into candies and fruit. The girl students who ate these 'showed an irresistable and otherwise inexplicable determination' to meet the man from whom the extracts were taken, and could single him out from a group of people.

In a book called *Magia Naturalis* by Johannes Baptista Porta, Peuckert discovered a formula for witches' salve, involving ingredients like thornapple *(datura stramonium)*, henbane *(hyoscyamus niger)* and deadly nightshade, as well as things like wild celery, parsley and lard (which should have been the fat of an unbaptised baby). In 1960, Peuckert and a fellow researcher applied the salve to their foreheads and armpits — and passed out. They woke twenty four hours later with blinding headaches and dry mouths — but both convinced they had attended a witches' Sabbat. Before comparing notes with his fellow researcher, Peuckert asked him to write down all he remembered of his dreams. He did the same. When the accounts were compared, there were astonishing similarities. Both had experienced dreams of flying, of landing on a mountain top, of wild sexual orgies with naked women, demons and monsters, perverted sex practices and paying homage to the Devil.

Why should the salve have produced the same dreams in two experimenters? Possibly because both were expecting something of the sort. Peuckert had also suggested that the salve may act upon specific sites in the brain, triggering images involved with sex and 'wickedness'. Dunning reports him as saying that witchcraft first emerged in the Middle Ages because this was when bands of gypsies introduced the necessary plants into northern Europe.

Peuckert's theories are reinforced by a recent book *Plants of the Gods* by Richard Schultes and Albert Hoffmann (the man who discovered LSD) which reveals that 'hallucinogenic drugs' can be manufactured from many plants that can be found in hedgerows, including deadly nightshade, the scotch rose, the male fern and the water lily.

Yet the mystery remains: why a particular salve should induce visions of Sabbats complete with demons. The answer may lie in a comment made by Aldous Huxley in his book about psychedelic drugs *Heaven and Hell:* that the mind, 'like the earth of a hundred years ago, has its darkest Africas, its unmapped Borneos and Amazonian basins' — an image that suggests that our inner worlds may have their own distinct geography. (This is, in fact, the essence of the system of magic known as Kabbalism.) Huxley goes on: 'Like the giraffe and the duck-billed platypus, the creatures inhabiting these remoter regions of the mind are exceedingly improbable.' As improbable as the demons and monsters seen by Dr Peuckert and his companion?

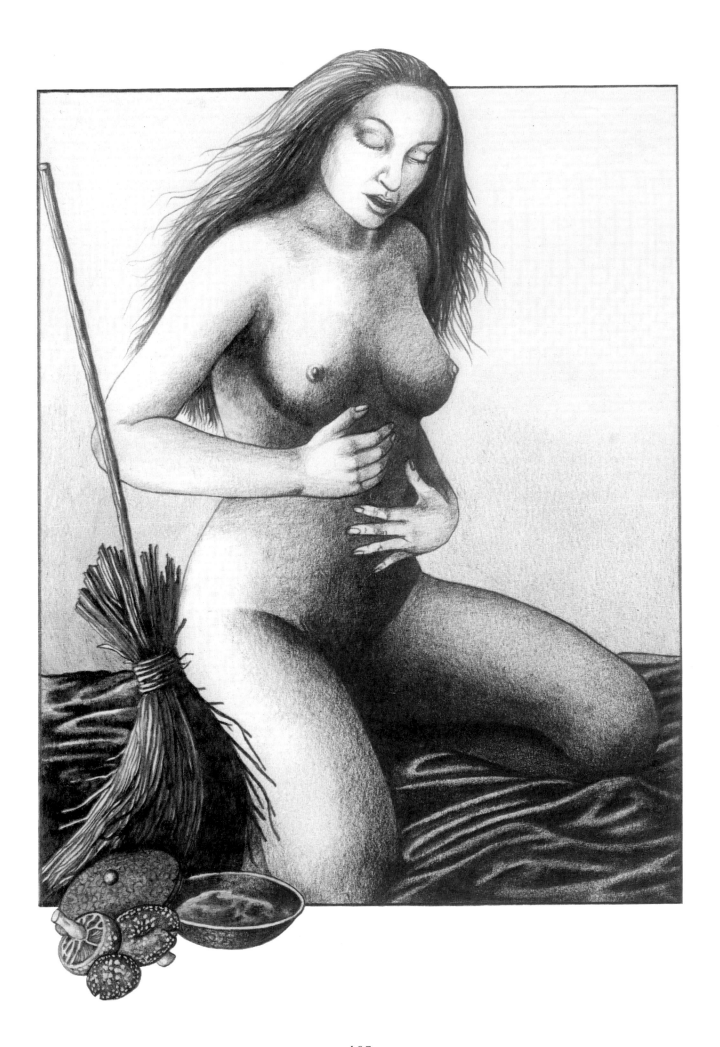

CHAPTER 21

Possession

Writers on witchcraft and demonology distinguish between 'obsession' and 'possession'. An obsessed person is simply 'haunted' by a demon or spirit; the possessed person is 'inhabited' by it. The view most widely held nowadays by psychical researchers is that a 'possessed' person is simply expressing an unconscious part of the personality which has been suppressed. This view is taken for granted in the best known of modern works on the subject, Aldous Huxley's *Devils of Loudun*. But the assumption may be questioned. Guy Playfair's book *This House Is Haunted* tells the story of the 'haunting' of the Harper family in Enfield by a poltergeist; the two daughters seemed to be the 'focus' of the manifestations. One day, the poltergeist had been making barking noises, which seemed to emanate from the girl named Janet. Playfair and his associate, Maurice Grosse, tried to persuade it to speak, and eventually, they succeeded in getting a growling voice which made comments like 'Shut up' and 'Fuck off '. The entity, which seemed to be speaking from Janet's mouth, named itself as Joe; a few days later, another one that called itself Bill Hobbs — and said it had lived in the house — spoke through Janet. This could not be described as 'mediumship', in which a person goes into a trance and is 'used' by the 'spirit'. Janet could ask the entity questions, which it answered promptly.

Poltergeists are thought to be mischief-making 'low-grade' entities feeding on surplus energies exuded by certain people.

Playfair is convinced that poltergeists are low grade entities' that cause mischief by somehow 'using' surplus energy exuded by certain people — usually adolescents. This does not exclude the possibility that there may also be some unconscious cooperation on the part of the 'focus', some basic discontent that expresses itself through the antics of the poltergeist. (The Enfield family was a 'broken home'.) If Playfair's theory is correct, then we cannot dismiss 'possession' as a form of unconscious exhibitionism, as Huxley does; (although Huxley does not deny the possibility of disembodied spirits or 'low grade entities').

The curious phenomenon of multiple personality — which laymen sometimes refer to incorrectly as schizophrenia — undoubtedly explains many cases of 'possession'. The French psychologist Pierre Janet described the remarkable case of a man called Achille, a French businessman, who first became 'dumb', then declared that he was in hell, that the Devil was inside him, and began to utter all kinds of blasphemies. Janet discovered that while Achille was speaking incoherently, he could insert a pencil petween Achille's fingers, and obtain written answers to questions. To the question 'Who are you?' he received the answer: 'The Devil'. Janet persuaded the 'Devil' to cause various hallucinations to his host, then asked him if he could send Achille to sleep. The Devil obligingly did so, whereupon Janet was able to ask Achille questions and receive answers — in effect, the 'Devil' had hypnotised him. Achille now admitted that he believed he was damned because he had, on one of his journeys away from home,committed a 'grave misdeed' — probably some 'perverse' act with a prostitute. Janet was able to cure Achille through hypnotic treatment, and by staging a scene in which Achille's wife forgave him. Here, then, is a case in which 'possession' can be explained purely in psychological terms.

In his account of the possessed nuns of Loudun, Rossell Hope Robbins rejects even the 'psychological' explanation, and declares that the nuns only pretended to be possessed in order to cause a downfall of the lecherous priest Urbain Grandier. The nuns went into violent convulsions, spoke in hoarse voices, and 'blasphemed' after the usual manner of demons. When Grandier himself was called in to exorcise them, they accused him of being the cause of their possession. In 1634, Grandier was tried and found guilty, and burned alive. But the possession of the nuns continued after his death.

In the case of the possessed nuns of Aix-en-Provence (1609-11), the 'focus' was a young nun, Madeleine de la Palud. She fell in love with her confessor, Father Louis Gaufridi, who seems to have been as much a 'man of the world' as Grandier, and began to go into convulsions, howling and blaspheming. Other nuns caught the 'infection'; Gaufridi was horribly tortured and burned, being first strangled.

CHAPTER 22

The Louvier Nuns

No case illustrates more strikingly the curious mixture of sexuality and religious emotion that lies at the root of witchcraft than that of the Louviers nuns.

Madeleine Bavent was an orphan who was born in Rouen in 1607, brought up by relatives, and apprenticed to a dressmaker. Together with other girls she sewed Church vestments; naturally, they saw a great deal of priests. One of these, a Franciscan named Fr Bonnetemps (a symbolically appropriate name) had already seduced three of the girls, and now did the same with Madeleine. Madeleine decided to enter a Franciscan convent — of St Louis and Elizabeth — at Louviers.

The convent had been founded recently — in 1616 — and if the later confessions of the nuns are to be accepted, was a hot-bed of vice from the beginning. The elderly priest, Fr David, was (according to Montague Summers) an adherent of the sect of Manichees — that is to say, a dualist who believed that this world is created by the Devil. (i.e. a Cathar.) But this hardly explains why he seems to have encouraged sexual licence, encouraging the nuns to walk around naked, and had no objection to their engaging in lesbian practices. Madeleine later declared that Fr David had habitually made her receive communion with breasts exposed. Rossell Hope Robbins states that the Louviers nuns received communion naked 'in token of poverty and humility'. But Madeleine later alleged that she and Fr David engaged in mutual masturbation, and that he was in the habit of fondling her indecently.

When Fr David died, his place was taken by Fr Mathurin Picard, who became chaplain in 1628, and his assistant, Fr Thomas Boullé. At her Easter confession, Fr Picard told Madeleine he loved her, and continued Fr David's practice of indecent caresses. Thereafter he made a habit of handling 'the most private parts of my body' during confession; he also raped her — or at least, forced intercourse on her — several times, so she became pregnant. As no mention is made of a child she presumably miscarried — possibly not through natural causes. She was only one of many nuns who were the mistresses of the priests.

In 1634, two sisters became 'possessed', writhing on the ground and foaming at the mouth, but the matter was hushed up. Picard died in 1642, and Boullé took over. Now the signs of demonic possession reappeared more violently than ever, with many nuns writhing and screaming on the ground. In the following year, the matter came to the attention of M. François Péricard, Bishop Evreux, and with the help of 'several Capuchin fathers of great experience', he began to investigate. Soon, the horrified priests were listening to incredible confessions of witches' Sabbats and intercourse with demons. Madeleine alleged that she was usually awakened before midnight — several nights a week — and conducted to a Sabbat in a nearby house. There a number of priests, sometimes dressed 'half as animals', performed a Black Mass, reading from a 'book of blasphemies', and performing various sexual rites with sacred wafers. She claimed that when everyone stabbed the Host with sharp knives, small drops of blood gathered underneath it. She also claimed that on one occasion, a woman brought her newly born baby, which was crucified. Two men who had come to watch were so horrified that they wanted to leave; they were not allowed to escape alive.

The nuns seem to have confessed to all these abominations, and laid the blame on Madeleine Bavent — who, together with the Mother Superior, seems to have been Picard's favourite. Madeleine declared that she had also been visited by the Devil in the form of a huge black cat, which she found sitting in her cell 'exhibiting a huge penis just like a man's'; when she tried to fly, it 'dragged me forcibly on the bed, and then violently ravished me, causing me to experience the most peculiar sensation'.

Madeleine was condemned as a witch and expelled from the convent; she was placed in an Ursuline convent in Rouen, where she attempted suicide, was treated with great harshness, and finally died in 1647 at the age of forty.

Boullé and several others — including priests — were arrested, and Boullé and another priest named Duval were publicly burned. The corpse of Fr Picard was exhumed and

burned. Two other priests were acquitted because the evidence against them came from convicted criminals. The nuns were scattered throughout other convents.

In retrospect it is hard to see what truth lies behind this incredible story. A Dr Yvelin, a royal physician, who examined the 'possessed' nuns, said he detected imposture and deceit, and thought they had been rehearsed for their exorcisms. Another witness declared that his evidence about the Black Mass had been suggested to him by the Bishop of Evreux. (He made this confession before being burned for heresy, so it seems likely that it was true.)

The likeliest explanation is that the nuns had been drawn piecemeal into corruption by Fr David, whom Robbins declares to have been a member of the Illuminati. This does not refer to the later sect founded by Adam Weishaupt, but to a sect of the late Middle Ages that believed that sex is a holy sacrament. It seems just possible that Fr David was a member of the 'Old Religion' of the moon goddess. (The mention of men dressed 'half as animals' suggests this.) Being younger and more virile, his successor Fr Picard made more active use of his opportunities. After Picard's death, some of the nuns convinced themselves that they were damned and — like Janet's patient Achille — began to suffer delusions. The Capuchin investigators, horrified by these tales of sexual orgies — possibly envious — felt that if the matter was to be dragged into open court, it would be preferable to involve the Devil and his legions, just to emphasise that everyone concerned was damned; otherwise, other convents might begin to find the whole tale morbidly fascinating.....

CHAPTER 23

Matthew Hopkins – The Rise and Fall of The Witchfinder General

The career of Matthew Hopkins had the effect of virtually ending the witchcraft persecution in England. Even the Revd. Montague Summers admits that his insincerity 'made his name stink in men's nostrils', and described him as 'the foulest of foul parasites, an obscene bird of prey..'

The career of Hopkins snowballed from his first denunciation of a witch in 1644. Hopkins was a not-particularly-successful lawyer, son of a clergyman, who moved to the small village of Mannningtree in Essex because he was unable to make a living in Ipswich. It was during the Civil War, East Anglia was on Cromwell's side, but tensions were considerable. In March 1644, Hopkins became convinced that there were witches who lived in Manningtree, and that they held meetings close to his house. He may possibly have been correct — country areas are full of witches. Hopkins decided that an old woman named Elizabeth Clarke was involved, and denounced her. She was arrested and stripped, to be searched for devil's marks. They discovered, apparently, something like a supernumerary teat. After being deprived of sleep for days, she confessed to suckling her familiars with it — a spaniel, a rabbit, a greyhound and a polecat. The witch fever spread through the village, and five other women were arrested. Four of these confessed readily to possessing familiars. Thirty two women were eventually thrown into jail, where four of them died. Twenty eight stood trial in a special court at Chelmsford.

Hopkins now had four assistants to help him in routing out witches, and no doubt this taste of power convinced him that he had discovered the road to fame and success. But it seems fairly certain that he was willing to perjure himself freely from the beginning — he asserted in court that he had seen Elizabeth Clarke's familiars, and his assistants backed him up. Nineteen women were hanged, on charges ranging from entertaining evil spirits to bewitching people to death. Five of these were reprieved, and the remaining eight were thrown back into jail for further investigations.

Before the Chelmsford trial was finished, Hopkins found himself greatly in demand. In times of war and public misfortune, distractions are welcomed. Hopkins moved around Essex, finding more witches, and accepting payment for his trouble; at Aldeburgh he was paid £6 for finding a witch, and at Stowmarket the local authorities paid him £23. In the days when a working wage was sixpence a day, these were large sums. During his year as witchfinder, Hopkins and his assistants made about £1,000, according to Summers. In Bury St Edmunds, he played his part in having two hundred people arrested; 68 of whom were hanged. He moved around Suffolk and Norfolk, finding witches in every place that invited him, and in a few that he selected for himself.

In April 1646, a Huntingdon clergyman named Gaule attacked Hopkins from the pulpit and published a pamphlet about his methods of 'torture'. Torture of witches was still forbidden by law in England, but Hopkins used other methods — 'pricking' for Devil's marks (areas the Devil had touched were supposed to be insensitive to pain), 'swimming' — which meant that the bound victim was tossed into a pond, and if she floated, she was innocent — and depriving of sleep for days on end, a method still used in 'brain washing'. The pamphlet was widely read, and it turned the tide against Hopkins. One historian of witchcraft relates that Hopkins was seized by an angry crowd and made to endure the water ordeal. He was in any case, a sick man. He retired to Manningtree, and died there later that year of tuberculosis.

Robbins estimates that Hopkins was responsible for several hundred hangings (witches in England were never burnt, although the North Berwick witches in Scotland were burned for having plotted against the king's person). And with his downfall, mass witch trials ceased in England.

CHAPTER 24

The Witches of Salem

The explosion of superstition and violence that occurred in Salem, Massachusetts, in 1692, is still one of the most puzzling episodes in American history. For most writers on the case — including Arthur Miller, who dramatised it in *The Crucible* — there is no mystery. A few bored and naughty children became obsessed by the voodoo tales of a black servant, and decided to pretend they were bewitched. Egged on by the local minister, a man of paranoid tendencies, they accused various people of witchcraft. The whole thing snowballed until over two hundred people were accused, twenty two of whom were executed or died in prison. Then, as suddenly as it began, the hysteria faded away. And the Salem witchcraft trials virtually ended the 'witchcraft craze' in America as the downfall of Matthew Hopkins ended it in England.

The case may not be as simple as it looks. Even Rossell Hope Robbins admits 'motives are very elusive'. Clearly, these children were not really 'bewitched'. But they behaved in some ways like the 'possessed' nuns of Loudun or Aix-en-Provence, or like some teenagers who are the 'focus' of poltergeist occurrences.

The Revd. Samuel Parris was not a popular man, for he seems to have been an unpleasant character, mean and bad tempered. He had brought with him from Barbados a number of black servants, including a woman called Tituba,

and her husband, 'John Indian'. During the long winter evenings, Tituba talked to the children about witches and spirits. His daughter Elizabeth, aged nine, her cousin Abigail Williams, aged eleven, and a friend called Ann Putnam, twelve, soon began behaving very oddly, having convulsions, screaming and talking disconnected nonsense. A doctor called in to 'cure' Elizabeth said he thought she was. bewitched. Other ministers were consulted, and decided that the devil was involved. Questioned — and beaten — by Parris, Tituba agreed that the devil had inspired her to 'work mischief' against the children, and named a pipe-smoking beggar woman named Sarah Good as an accomplice. The children also mentioned Sarah Good as well as a bedridden old woman, Sarah Osborne. When a magistrate named Hathorne asked the girls about their convulsions, they began to moan with pain, and declared that the 'spirit' (or spectre) of Sarah Good was biting and pinching them. Sarah Good and Sarah Osborne both denied in court that they knew anything about witchcraft, but Tituba admitted it all with a certain relish; she went on expanding her confessions for three days. Tituba declared that Sarah Good and Sarah Osborne had been present at a witches' Sabbat, and added that there were two more local women whom she did not know. This caused widespread gossip and speculation. Twelve year old Ann Putnam put an end to this by declaring that one of the witches was a woman called Martha Cory — who had laughed unbelievingly when the girls threw their convulsions — and that the other was a saintly old lady named Rebecca Nurse. A farmer named Proctor — another sceptic — was also accused.

The whole area was now in the grip of a witchcraft scare; people were afraid to go out after dark because witches were supposed to be able to turn themselves into animals or night birds — a remnant of legends of werewolves and vampires. Eight more local children became 'afflicted' and screamed out the names of 'witches' who were tormenting them. A woman named Bridget Bishop — who had a reputation for being 'fast' — was tried and executed in June 1692. Sarah Osborne died in prison, but Sarah Good was tried and executed, together with four others, in July. A minister named George Burroughs was denounced, and he was also tried and executed.

The more hysteria increased, the more the girls — now eleven of them — seemed to be tormented by devils. By September, the death toll had increased to twenty, and one unfortunate man — Giles Corey — was literally pressed to death under enormous weights in an effort to force him to confess. He refused (although it would have saved his life) because his goods would have been forfeit to the state, and he had no intention of dying a pauper. His wife was hanged as a witch.

The various girls were called to neighbouring towns to

identify witches, and it looked as if the trials and executions would spread to Andover and Boston. The Andover magistrate declined to sign more than forty warrants and had to flee with his wife to escape being tried as a witch. Then the girls began to overreach themselves. They named the wife of the governor, Sir William Phips, as a witch, and the president of Harvard College; the magistrates told them sternly that they were mistaken, and this was the beginning of the end of the persecutions. When Governor Phips returned from fighting Indians on the Canadian border, he dismissed the court and released many of the accused. In further trials, 'spectral evidence' — the notion that the disembodied spirits of witches could torment their victims — was disallowed, and only three people out of fifty two were condemned. Phips reprieved them, released all others from prison, and the Salem craze ended abruptly about a year after it began. One of the girls Ann Putnam, later confessed that she had been 'deluded by Satan' when she accused Rebecca Nurse and others. The Reverend Parris, now attacked and denounced, left Salem with his family. Abigail Williams, according to legend, became a prostitute.

Even Montague Summers agrees that the Salem trials were the result of hysteria and the 'diseased imaginings of neurotic children'. But he was convinced that there *is* positive evidence of involvement in witchcraft in a few of the cases. It seems probable that George Burroughs, Bridget Bishop and Martha Carrier were members of a coven — although they had nothing to do with 'bewitching' the children.

And what about the children? All writers on the affair assume that they were mischievous, 'prankish', and that the whole thing snowballed out of a harmless game. But what was this game? The answer, fairly certainly, is some form of 'magic'. Tituba was familiar with voodoo and obeah. And the essence of voodoo rituals — as David St Clair emphasises in *Drum and Candle* and Guy Playfair in *The Flying Cow* — is the evocation of 'low grade' spirits to do the bidding of the magician. The three children, bored with the long winter in the dreary New England village, undoubtedly 'tried out' what Tituba had taught them. Their intentions were harmless enough — rather like a modern child playing with an ouija board or automatic writing. But two of them at least were at the dangerous age when children become the focus of poltergeist phenomena — Ann Putnam was twelve and looked older. We do not know very much about 'possession', and the usual theory is that it is pure hysteria; but again, anyone who takes the trouble to read T.K.Oesterreich's classic *Possession:Demoniacal and Other,* or Martin Ebon's anthology *Exorcism: Fact not Fiction* will see that there is a very thin dividing line between 'possession' and being a focus of poltergeist activity.

CHAPTER 25

The Chambre Ardente Affair

In France, as in England and America, the witchcraft craze blew itself out in a storm of extraordinary violence. In England it was the hysteria instigated by Matthew Hopkins, in America, the affair of the Salem witches. In France, it was the Chambre Ardente scandal.

In 1673, during the reign of Louis the Fourteenth, two priests informed the police in Paris that a number of penitents had asked absolution for murdering their spouses. No names were mentioned, because of the secrecy of the confessional, but it alerted the Chief of Police, Nicholas de la Reynie. What was happening, it seemed, was that a ring of fortune tellers and 'sorcerers' were supplying 'succession powders' — a euphemism for poisons — to wealthy men and women who preferred lovers to matrimonial entanglements.

De la Reynie could only keep his ear to the ground. It took him four years to fit together the clues that led him to the recognition that there was an international 'poisons ring' — much as there are now drugs rings — headed by men of influence. A remark of a fortune teller, Marie Bosse, about being about to retire when she had arranged three more poisonings, provided the lead he had been waiting for. A disguised policewoman consulted Marie Bosse on how she could get rid of her husband, and made an arrest when she was sold poison. Many poisons were found in Marie Bosse's house. She and her husband and two sons were arrested; also,

121

another fortune teller known as La Vigoreux, who shared a communal bed with the family.

Interrogations began to reveal the names of their customers, and the revelation shocked the King. It seemed that half the aristocracy were trying to poison one another, and that two ladies had even approached another fortune teller for means of getting rid of one of his own mistresses Louise de la Vallière.

But this was not simply a matter of murder or attempted murder. The customers were also convinced that the fortune tellers could produce charms and magic potions to secure the affections of their admirers, and apparently had no objection if the Devil was involved.

Stern and decisive action was called for — after all, the king might be the next victim... He created a special commission, a kind of star chamber, which sat in a room draped in black curtains and lit with candles — hence the Chambre Ardente — lighted (or burning) chamber.

What made it so frightening was that the methods of poisoning were so subtle. A Madame de Poulaillon, who wanted to kill her aged husband so she could marry her young lover, had been impregnating his shirts with arsenic, which would cause symptoms similar to those of syphilis; she would then rub the sores with a 'healing ointment' that would kill him in ten weeks — and there would be no suspicion.

The chief defendants were Marie Bosse, La Vigoreux, an abortionist known as La Lepère, and a well known fortune teller called Catherine Deshayes, known as La Voisin. La Vigoreux and Marie Bosse were quickly condemned — on May 6, 1678 — to be burnt alive and one son, François Bosse, hanged. La Voisin was horribly tortured, and, when she refused to confess to poisoning, burnt alive in an iron chair — Mme de Sevigné described in a letter how the old woman cursed violently and threw off the straw half a dozen times, until the flames became too strong and she disappeared in them.

All this was kept secret; one reason being that the king's mistress Mme de Montespan was deeply involved. And more investigation revealed that various priests had performed Black Masses and even sacrificed babies to the Devil. A hunchback, the Abbé Guibourg used as an altar the naked body of a woman, placing the chalice on her belly; Mme de Montespan had often served as the altar. A baby would then be sacrificed by having its throat cut, and the body thrown into an oven. La Voisin confessed at her trial that she had disposed of two thousand five hundred babies like this. On another occasion, Mme des Oillets came to make a charm for the king, accompanied by a man. The priest said that sperm from both was necessary, but since Mme des Oillets was menstruating, he accepted a few drops of menstrual blood from her, while the man masturbated into the chalice.

Many other priests proved to be involved, and it became clear that an alarming number of churchmen had no objections to dealings with the Devil. One had consecrated a stone altar in a brothel, another strangled a baby after baptising it with oil reserved for Extreme Unction, another copulated with the girl who was serving as an altar in full view of his audience; another fortune teller described how she had sacrificed her own new born baby at a black mass.

By 1680, it had struck the king that a full-scale scandal could lead to unforeseen results, since so many nobles were involved. He decided to suspend the Chambre Ardente. No noblemen — or women — were sentenced, but de la Reynie continued to arrest and torture fortune tellers. A hundred and four people were sentenced: thirty six to death, others to slavery in the galleys or banishment. The chief result of the case was that fortune tellers were banned by law, and witchcraft was declared to be a superstition. After that, people accused of witchcraft were sent to a madhouse, the Salpêtrière. In fact, a man was executed in Bordeaux in 1718 for causing a man to become impotent and his wife barren; but then, working 'fancied acts of magic' was still a hanging offence.

Louis attempted to suppress all the evidence for the affair in 1709 by ordering all papers to be destroyed; but the official transcripts were overlooked.

It seems ironical that the last major witchcraft trial in France — virtually in Europe — should have been a case in which there seems to be abundant evidence of genuine 'black magic' practices. It inevitably raises the suspicion that in at least a percentage of early witchcraft trials, the evidence about Sabbats and black masses may have been less imaginary than we now assume.

CHAPTER 26

The Birth of Spiritualism

'Modern Spiritism is merely Witchcraft revived' says the Revd. Montague Summers severely. He intended it as a condemnation; yet in another sense it may be taken simply as a statement of fact.

'Spiritualism' began on March 31, 1848, in the house of the Fox family of Hydesville, New York. The family had been disturbed by rapping noises, and on this evening, the two daughters asked the invisible knocker to repeat noises made by snapping their fingers; it obliged. Later it answered with a code of one knock for yes, two for no. The case caused a widespread sensation. Other people found that they could produce rapping noises by addressing a request to 'spirits'. Others discovered that if they went into a trance, 'spirits' would speak through their mouths. The movement swept across America, and quickly spread to Europe. It was assumed that the the spirits of the dead were communicating, and that this proved that the soul survives after death; as a result, 'spiritualism' was soon established as a church.

It is clear that what happened in the home of the Fox sisters is what would now be called poltergeist manifestations. It is true that the 'spirit' declared itself (through a code of raps) to be the ghost of a murdered peddler; but he was never traced. In general, poltergeists seem to have little in common with the spirits that manifest themselves at seances, and which claim to be spirits of the dead. Sceptics insist that

126

this is self deception, or at best, unconscious telepathy on the part of the 'medium'; and in many cases, this is probably so. There remain a small residue of cases that do not seem to admit of this explanation.

But what *is* clear is that 'spiritualism' is basically a revival of the shamanism of our remote ancestors — in which the *shaman* went into a trance and 'communicated' with the spirit world — and that the 'spirits' that cause poltergeist effects are the 'demons' that witches invoked with their spells and rituals. It makes no difference whether we regard poltergeists as a manifestation of the unconscious mind, or as some kind of 'low-grade spirit' with a taste for mischief; their antics bear a strong family resemblance to those of the imps and demons of the witchcraft trials. So in a basic sense, Summers was correct. Spiritualism was a rediscovery of certain 'forces' that had been regarded as 'demonic' in the days when all good Christians believed in demons and malign spirits.

In which case, the 'commonsense' view of witchcraft taken by nearly all modern writers on the subject — Rossell Hope Robbins in the *Encyclopedia of Witchcraft*, Trevor-Roper in *The European Witch Craze of the 16th and 17thCenturies*, Keith Thomas in *Religion and the Decline of Magic* is quite simply unacceptable. The Dominican Inquisitors may have been superstitious bigots; but at least they recognised that our universe is pervaded by unknown forces.

The Fox sisters.

CHAPTER 27

Madam Blavatsky

Helena Petrovna Blavatsky, founder of the Theosophical Society, was condemned in her own time as a fraud; yet she undoubtedly possessed powers that would have caused her to be classified as a witch in earlier times. A young disciple, Charles Johnston, quotes a typical example. Madame Blavatsky was sitting at a card table, playing patience, Johnston sitting opposite. Growing tired of her game, she began to drum idly on the table with her fingertips; then 'drawing her hand back a foot or so from the table, she continued the tapping movements in the air. The taps, however, were still perfectly audible — on the table, a foot from her hand. I could both feel and hear them. It was something like taking sparks from the prime conductor of an electric machine.. then she changed her direction again and began to bring the taps to bear on the top of my head. They were quite audible and, needless to say, I felt them quite distinctly. I was at the opposite side of the table, some five or six feet away, all through this little experiment in the unexplained laws of nature, and the psychical powers latent in man.'

The first time Madame Blavatsky met her disciple Sinnett, he remarked that he had tried spiritualism, but could not even get a rap. 'Oh, raps are the easiest to get' said Madame Blavatsky, and the room suddenly resounded with them.

She also apparently possessed one of the traditional of

powers of 'witches', second sight. At Simla, in India, she placed a sealed letter against her forehead and was able to state the name of the writer correctly. She asked her hostess, a Mrs Hume, if she wanted anything 'materialised'. Mrs Hume mentioned an old family brooch which she had lost some years before. Madame Blavatsky stared intently at Mrs Hume then said that it would not be in the house but in the garden — was there in the garden a flowerbed shaped like a star? There was. They all trooped into the garden with lanterns, uprooted several flowers, and found the brooch wrapped in paper. Madame Blavatsky wanted her hosts to understand that her mysterious 'Brothers' had materialised it; but it seems more likely that she used some form of 'second sight' — many dowsers have the same ability — to locate it.

During discussion with some pandits (scholars), Madame Blavatsky got impatient with a German who remarked that the yogis of old had remarkable powers — they could make roses fall from the air. 'Oh, they say that, do they?' said Madame Blavatsky irritably. She muttered certain words under her breath and swept her hand through the air; roses fell on the heads of the company.

Later, as they were all about to leave, Colonel Olcott noticed on Madame Blavatsky's face 'that strange look of power which almost always preceded a phenomenon'. She took the lamp in one hand, pointed her other finger at the flame and said: 'Go up'. It rose to the top of the chimney. 'Go down'. The flame sank again. (The story would have been even more impressive if Madame Blavatsky had not been holding the lamp.)

So Madame Blavatsky was certainly a 'witch' — one who happened to be born with certain odd powers, which she took the trouble to develop. (That she possessed such powers does not mean of course, that we must take Theosophy seriously — this must depend on the individual reader's assessment of books like *Isis Unveiled*.) What is worth bearing in mind is that Madame Blavatsky was a very powerful personality, and her biographies (such as the excellent one by John Symonds) give the impression that her 'powers' were in some respect an overflow of sheer vitality. But it should also be noted that she herself always insisted that her 'effects' were produced with the aid of the 'secret masters' or Brothers — reminding us that the majority of witches believe their powers derive from 'spirits'. Study of the life of Madame Blavatsky could provide an insight into what really happened in remote country villages in the days of what Rossell Hope Robbins insists on calling 'the witchcraft delusion'.

Overleaf Madame Blavatsky manifesting roses from thin air.

CHAPTER 28

The Golden Dawn

The Hermetic Order of the Golden Dawn belongs to the tradition of cabbalistic magic (discussed in the chapter on Magic and Magicians) and so is only indirectly related to the subject of this book. Witchcraft seems to be a more — or — less natural faculty — like 'second sight' — which is based upon the assumption that there are invisible powers or spirits that can be persuaded to carry out simple tasks. Magic depends on the assumption that there is another order of reality that lies beyond our senses, and that the magician can, by careful preparation, gain a certain limited access to this reality.

According to its original members, the Golden Dawn originated in 1885 when a clergyman named Woodford found a dusty handwritten manuscript on a secondhand bookstall in Farringdon Street, London. It proved to be written in code, and to contain five magical rituals for initiating members into a secret society. There was also a letter declaring that anyone interested in these rituals should contact a certain Fraülein Sprengel in Stuttgart. It was Fraülein Sprengel who gave Dr Wynn Wescott, another student of the Kabbalah, permission to found a magical society, which was at first called the Isis-Urania Temple of the Golden Dawn.

Unfortunately, this tale is almost certainly an invention, as Ellic Howe reveals in his book on the Golden Dawn. It was intended simply to endow the newly formed society with a certain mystique. Equally dubious was the character of the most important founder member of the Order, Samuel Liddell Mathers, son of a commercial clerk from Hackney, who liked to call himself MacGregor Mathers or the Comte de Glenstrae, and whose passion for dominating his fellow members finally led to the break up of the Order. Yet it would be a mistake to dismiss the Golden Dawn as a mixture of chicanery and wishful thinking. For all his eccentricity and capacity for grandiose self-deception, Mathers was a genuine scholar, whose knowledge of Kabbalism was enormous. The hermetic tradition (magic is supposed to derive from its mysterious founder, Hermes Trismegistos) is based upon the notion that magic makes use of certain forces in the universe, and that this can be done by a total amateur and unbeliever if he follows the correct procedures, just as an unbeliever could make a magnet by following the correct procedures. The 'forces' involved are basically the natural forces exerted by the heavenly bodies on the earth. Magic also assumes that the 'unconscious' powers of the human psyche are far greater than we realise. And these are, in fact, the assumptions of modern primitive *shamans*, and it seems probable that they were held by our Stone Age ancestors.

The poet W.B. Yeats was one of the early members of the Golden Dawn — coming to it after an interest in Madame Blavatsky and Theosophy. In an important essay on magic, Yeats describes a 'magical operation' by Mathers and his wife in which Mathers was able to induce curious visions, which were seen by all present.

The poet W.B. Yeats was one of the early members of the Golden Dawn — coming to it after an interest in Madame Blavatsky and Theosophy. In an important essay on magic, Yeats describes a 'magical operation' by Mathers and his wife in which Mathers was able to induce curious visions, which were seen by all present.

Magic, as practised in the Golden Dawn, depended upon the assumption that the human will can be trained and concentrated until it can exert 'paranormal' effects, and that this will must be directed and stimulated by imagination. The members of the Order accepted that the various 'realms' — orders of reality — described in the Kabbalah are real, and that these can also be explored by a process of inner-vision, what might be regarded as a kind of controlled dreaming while awake. (It is worth noting that many exponents of 'astral projection' — in which the spirit is supposed to leave the body — believe that it can be achieved by *realising* you are asleep and dreaming.) Mathers' magic almost certainly worked *because* he was a humourless obsessive with delusions of grandeur. Yeats, with his wider intelligence, lacked the single-mindedness to become a good magician.

Another basic notion of the Golden Dawn was that

certain symbols or ideas have a deep — and objective — meaning for all human beings — that, for example, if someone places a piece of cardboard containing a water symbol against his forehead and allows the imagination to work, he will see water in various forms — but by no conceivable accident, fire or earth. In the 20th century, this theory has been given a certain intellectual respectability by the theories of Jung about archetypes and universal symbols.

By 1898, the Golden Dawn was already being torn apart by a power struggle. Westcott regarded himself as the leader; but Mathers felt the position should be rightfully his. He claimed to be in touch with 'secret chiefs' (rather like Madame Blavatsky's secret brotherhood) who dictated new rituals through the mediumship of his wife. But even though Westcott resigned (when his employer, the London County Council, intimated that magic was not a respectable hobby for a coroner), the wrangles continued, and Golden Dawn broke up thirteen years after it was founded. Offshoots continued to exist, one run by a learned American, A.E. Waite who wrote a number of unreadable books on such subjects as the Kabbalah and the Holy Grail, another by the actress Florence Farr and the novelist Arthur Machen, while in the 1920s, a young occultist named Dion Fortune used Golden Dawn rituals obtained from Mrs Mathers after the death of her husband (in the flu epidemic of 1918) to found an order called the Society of the Inner Light. She later lived in Glastonbury — where Margaret Murray had stumbled upon her theory that witches are members of an old fertility religion; so that the town once identified with King Arthur also has its historical links with witchcraft and with traditional magic. In 1934, Israel Regardie an ex-member of yet another offshoot of the Golden Dawn, the Stella Matutina, published all its 'secret rituals', enraging members and effectively destroying the Order, yet earning the gratitude of historians and students of magic, whose number has continued to increase.

Overleaf Accolytes of The Golden Dawn.

133

CHAPTER 29

Aleister Crowley

Like MacGregor Mathers (see chapter on the Golden Dawn) Aleister Crowley was the possessor of a very considerable ego. His first love was literature — 'a strange coincidence', he once remarked, 'that one small county should have given England her two greatest poets — for one must not forget Shakespeare'. But in spite of the tongue-in-cheek self-aggrandisement, he knew that he would never be a poet of the first rank. Magic was a second-best. Yet precisely because he was driven by a compulsive desire to be recognised, he became a very considerable 'magician'.

Edward Alexander Crowley was born on October 12, 1875, in Leamington, Warwickshire, the son of a retired brewer who had become a devoted member of the Plymouth Brethren. Crowley had the temperament of a spoilt brat, and joyless religious background in his home increased his natural rebelliousness. Yet he enormously admired his father, whose death when Crowley was eleven increased his natural wildness. A highly religious uncle deepened his Swinburnian hatred of Christianity, and he took pleasure in smoking in the lavatory; he also seduced — or allowed himself to be seduced by — a maidservant on his mother's bed, while his mother was at church. For Crowley, sex was always a symbol of delicious wickedness. At Trinity College, Cambridge, he wrote poetry — which he published at his own expense — and a sadistic pornographic novel in the manner of Sade.

Crowley carried with him all his life a schoolboyish desire to 'shock the bourgeoisie'.

Mathers' translation of three books of the Zohar, *The Kabbalah Unveiled,* excited him, as did a work on ceremonial magic by A.E.Waite. In a hotel room in Stockholm he 'was awakened to the knowledge that I possessed a magical means of becoming conscious and of satisfying a part of my nature which had up to that moment concealed itself from me'. He wrote to Waite, and in 1898, became a member of the Golden Dawn. The struggle for power was already going on within its leadership, and Crowley took the side of Mathers — although two such self-obsessed characters could not have remained allies indefinitely. In the following year, Crowley (who was a wealthy young man) rented a house at Boleskin, on the shore of Loch Ness, and proceeded to practise the magic of Abramelin the Mage — the first aim of which is to establish contact with one's 'Holy Guardian Angel'. Crowley claims that the house filled with shadowy shapes, and that the lodgekeeper went mad and tried to kill his wife. This may well be true; attempts to 'summon' spirits are quite likely to succeed, although the results may be thoroughly unpredictable, like inviting a crowd of juvenile delinquents into your home.

During the next few years Crowley did a great deal of globe-trotting, practising magic in various hotel rooms on his travels — and spending a large part of his private fortune. Back in England, he married the sister of the painter Gerald Kelly, a highly neurotic and unstable girl named Rose, who then joined him in his globe-trotting. In Cairo, Rose showed signs of being a medium, and Crowley finally achieved contact with his guardian angel, who was called Aiwass, and at his dictation, took down a work called *The Book of the Law*, which Crowley regarded as an immense revelation. The book bears the marks of having originated in Crowley's own unconscious mind; it is full of a hedonism reminiscent of Wilde, and an anti-moralism that sounds like Nietzsche's *Thus Spake Zarathustra*. 'Do what thou wilt shall be the whole of the law'. Like Dostoevsky's Raskolnikov, Crowley seemed to feel that if God does not exist, then man must become God, and must prove it by doing whatever he wants to. The principle led him into a great deal of trouble during his lifetime.

In Paris in 1904 Crowley wrote to Mathers declaring that the 'Secret Chiefs' (with whom Mathers claimed to be in touch) had appointed him head of the Golden Dawn. Mathers ignored the letter and the men became enemies. But when Crowley began publishing various secret rituals of the Golden Dawn in a periodical work called *The Equinox*, Mathers obtained a legal injunction to restrain him. Back at Boleskin, Crowley claims that Mathers launched a magical

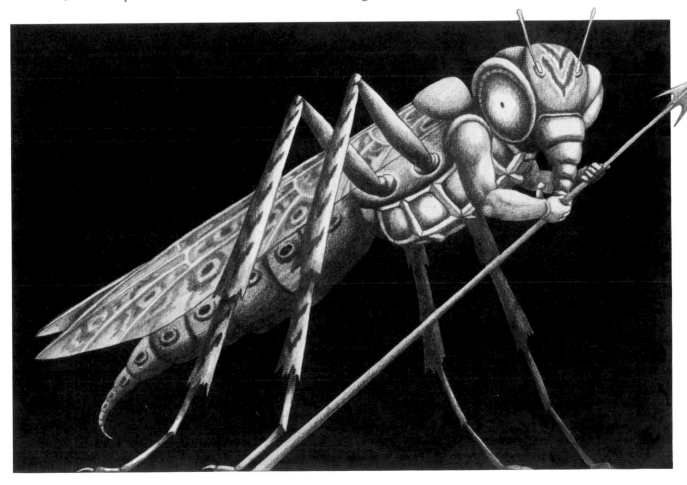

attack on him, killing most of the dogs and making the servants ill. He retaliated with talismans from Abramelin the Mage, invoking Beelzebub and his forty-nine servitors. ('I may mention: Nimorup, a stunted dwarf with large head and ears. His lips are greeny bronze and slobbery. Nominon, a large red spongey jelly-fish with one greenish luminous spot like a nasty mess. Holastri, an enormous pink bug..') Because of Mathers, a workman 'became maniacal' and attacked Rose. But 'as soon as Beelzebub got on the job, the magical assaults ceased...'

In 1912, a German magical order called the Ordo Templis Orientis accused Crowley of giving away one of their basic secrets — that sex could be used for magical purposes; they ended by authorising Crowley to form his own English branch of the Order, and Crowley's later magical diaries show that he practised sexual magic assiduously, using both male and female disciples in the 'operations'.

During the first world war, Crowley went to America and disseminated anti-British propaganda. It was a period of poverty and humiliation. In fact, the remainder of Crowley's life was a struggle to maintain himself in the style to which he had become accustomed (he had no compunction about living off friends or mistresses for as long as they would put up with it). After the war, he used a legacy of £3,000 to buy a farmhouse in Cefalù, which he renamed The Abbey of Theleme (*thelema* being a reference to Rabelais's 'Do what you will..') and ran a kind of magical *ashram* there, with bowls of cocaine out on the tables so guests could take a pinch at will. (Crowley was convinced that he was strong-minded enough to enjoy cocaine without becoming an addict, but proved to be mistaken — by the end of his life, his daily dose of drugs would have killed several normal men.) He had a number of mistresses, the current favourite always being known as the Scarlet Woman, and went out of his way to seduce any women who came to stay. His magical journal has entries like this: 'Marie Maddingley, respectable married woman..the girl is very weak, feminine, easily excitable and very keen, it being the first time she has committed adultery. Operation highly orgiastic, and elixir [i.e. sperm obtained in this way] of first rate quality...' You can almost hear Crowley rolling the word 'adultery' round his mouth. This adolescent obsession with 'wickedness' remained with him all his life, a legacy of his puritanical upbringing.

In 1923, a scandal made the Italian government order him out of Cefalù — a disciple named Loveday died after being made to drink the blood of a cat Crowley had 'sacrificed'.

Crowley died in 1947, but the last twenty years of his life were something of an anticlimax. He thoroughly enjoyed all the publicity about being 'the wickedest man in the

world' — outcome of the Cefalù scandal — it was 'fame at last' — but it did him little practical good, making him widely disliked and misunderstood. He wrote an immense autobiography, the *Confessions* — which he typically referred to as the 'autohag' — a hagiography being the life of a saint — and two interesting novels, *Moonchild* and *Confessions of a Drug Fiend* (the catchpenny title indicating how urgently he needed money). He even plotted with a friend, Nina Hamnett, to sue her for a 'libel' in her autobiography *Laughing Torso,* to extort money (which they would share) from her publisher; it rebounded against him when the defence described Crowley's magical activities and the judge found against him.

John Symonds, who knew Crowley in his last years — when he was drug addict living in Hastings — describes him in a book called *The Magic of Aleister Crowley,* and Crowley emerges as a mild, harmless, rather pathetic old gentleman, a 'decadent' who had long outlived his period. He died in 1947, and there was a scandal when his *Hymn to Pan* was read at the funeral service.

Yet anyone who turns with exasperation from John Symonds' account of Crowley (in *The Great Beast*) to his magical writings will discover that here was a mind of considerable power. He is, unfortunately, always capable of silliness — usually when carried away by a desire to get his own back on someone — yet his writings on magic, the Kabbalah, the Tarot, and other esoteric matters, are very remarkable indeed. Many modern students of the hermetic arts regard *Magick in Theory and Practice* as one of the two cornerstones of modern magical theory, the other being Dion Fortune's book *The Mystical Qabalah.* (One practising magician tells me that the book should be used with care as it is 'booby trapped' — Crowley always had a sadistic sense of humour.) Israel Regardie's books about Crowley (like *The Eye in the Triangle*) should also be read by those who want to understand what was best and most serious about Crowley. A volume made up of his letters to a female correspondent, *Magick Without Tears,* is an excellent introduction to the best and worst of Crowley.

Crowley undoubtedly possessed strange powers. His definition of magic was 'the Science and Art of causing change to occur in conformity with the will'. Because of his overdeveloped ego, his 'magical will' was formidable. In Cefalù, he was able to order a cat to 'freeze' and remain in the same place for hours before sacrificing it. He demonstrated his powers in a New York street by falling into step behind a man, then suddenly buckling at the knees — causing the man to collapse on the pavement. Oliver Wilkinson has described how Crowley 'bewitched' two men, causing one to lose consciousness, the other to drop on all fours and behave like a dog.★ This kind of 'magic' obviously has much in common with the curious feats of Wolf Messing.

★See my *Mysteries,* P. 489.

140

CHAPTER 30

Gerald Gardner and The Modern Witchcraft Revival

Like Crowley, Gerald Gardner — the man most responsible for the modern witchcraft revival — was a man whose personal character will hardly stand close analysis.

Born in June, 1884, he was an asthmatic child whose upbringing was left largely in the hands of an Irish nanny whose spankings gave him a lifelong taste for being flogged. His father was a wealthy but eccentric timber merchant who would remove all his clothes at the slightest sign of rain and sit in it until it stopped. Gardner travelled a great deal in childhood and youth, particularly in the Canaries and North Africa, and developed an obsession with knives, probably connected with his sado-masochism. He followed a number of professions — among them rubber planter and customs officer and when he retired to England at the age of 52, in 1936, took up nudism and became a member of the Folk Lore Society. He was also interested in spiritualism.

He achieved fame quite suddenly at the age of seventy with the publication, in 1954, of *Witchcraft Today*, which 'revealed' that witchcraft covens were still flourishing all over the place. (Theda Kenyon had said as much in *Witches Still Live* as long ago as 1931, but no one had paid much attention.) An introduction by Professor Margaret Murray lent it a certain respectability — although by this period, she herself was under attack for her views on the 'Old Religion' and its continuance down the ages. Gardner supported her theory, and insisted that witchcraft, as widely practised today, is merely a harmless fertility religion whose purpose is to make the earth fruitful. What excited the journalists, and earned Gardner the title 'king of the witches', was his admission that he was a member of a coven, and the hints that soon followed that these covens practised sexual rites, including ritual flagellation (inevitably), the fivefold kiss (when the High Priestess kisses the Priest on the lips, breast and genitals) and the Great Rite when the Priest and Priestess copulate before the coven.

Gardner died ten years later, not long before his eightieth birthday, on a ship bound for North Africa, and a witchcraft museum he owned at Castletown on the Isle of Man was taken over by a witch named Monique Wilson, together with her husband. (It had been founded originally by Cecil Williamson, who subsequently founded another at Boscastle in Cornwall).

Like Mathers and Crowley, Gardner was something of a fantasist; he sometimes wore a kilt, and claimed to trace his ancestry back to an' aristocratic ancestor named Simon Le Gardinor in 1379. In *The Authors and Writers Who's Who* of 1963 he is described as 'Ph.D' and 'D.Litt', and to have been privately educated; in fact, he told his biographer, Jack L. Bracelin, that he taught himslf to read from issues of the *Strand Magazine* while travelling, and he certainly never attended a university. (The membership list of the Folk Lore Society also mentions an M.A.) A paper he read to the Folk Lore Society on the development of Manx fishing craft was lifted without acknowledgement from earlier published papers.

The journalist Frank Smyth, who has written about Gardner, admits that he has no idea of whether Gardner invented the modern witch cult, or only revealed its existence. With the repeal of the Witchcraft Act in England in 1951, witchcraft finally ceased to be illegal. (It had still been used occasionally in the 20th century to prosecute mediums suspected of fraud.) There is little recent evidence of witch covens in England before Gardner. But within five years of the publication of *Witchcraft Today,* there were dozens, and by the mid-1960s, there were probably hundreds spread across England and America — pictures of naked men and women trooping around in circles or performing rituals with swords can be found in every illustrated book on witchcraft of the past quarter of a century.

Gardner insists that witches should be regarded as modern descendants of the Druids. 'Is it possible for witches to do people harm?' he asks, and answers: 'I can only say that I have not known them try. I know no spells to this end...' This is being disingenuous. If — as he insists — witches possess healing powers, then it seems logical that these powers could be used to do the opposite. In *Witches Still Live*, Theda Kenyon — who is also anxious to insist that most

witchcraft is 'white' — nevertheless mentions the case of an Aberdeen witch who was always consulted when children or cattle fell ill, and had never been known to do harm, lost her temper with a man who threw her off his land and then put a spell on his five children — adding quickly: 'It is notable that this evil spell was in the nature of a reprisal — not the opening of hostilities'. T.C. Lethbridge, one of the most eminent of modern writers on paranormal subjects, had no doubt about the harmfulness of black magic; when his neighbour — a Devon witch — told him that she proposed to put a spell on a neighbouring farmer with whom she was quarrelling, he warned her that it could bounce back. In fact, the cattle of two other nearby farmers became ill, and the 'witch' died under curious circumstances that looked like murder. In the encyclopedia *Man, Myth and Magic*, a photographer named Serge Kordeiv described how he became a member of a Gardneresque coven, and how his luck changed abruptly for the better soon after he joined, then became appalling after he decided to leave.

A journalist friend, Colin Cross, told me of a similar experience. He had interviewed a well-known British witch for a colour supplement article, and had made some sarcastic comment about the money she made by selling love potions; the witch told him she had cursed him. For the next six months, he claims, his luck changed abruptly for the worse, and everything that *could* go wrong did.

Crowley or Mathers would have found the whole question naive. For them, magic meant making use of certain natural forces through the discipline of the will; therefore, it could be used to curse as easily as to heal or bless.

Right Modern witch at her altar with her ritual tools.

CHAPTER 31

The Death of Jayne Mansfield

On the evening of July 29, 1967, a middle aged man suddenly collapsed on the floor of his San Francisco apartment; and as his wife and son bent over him, a woman's voice came out of his mouth, screaming: 'I don't want to die'. Both claimed they recognised the voice as that of actress Jayne Mansfield, who happened to be a member of the same congregation. They later learned that Jayne Mansfield had died that evening; she had been in a car with her attorney — and lover — when a truck hurtled from under a narrow bridge and crashed into their car; Jayne Mansfield was decapitated.

The 'congregation' of which Jayne Mansfield was a member was not a normal Christian church; it was the Church of Satan, run by an ex-police photographer, Anton Szandor LaVey.

Born in 1930, of Hungarian stock, LaVey claims that he decided 'the Bible was wrong' when he was twelve. When he left college he worked for a while in a circus as an animal trainer, then as a 'magician' and hypnotist. In the 1960's LaVey became interested in ritual magic and began holding weekly meetings. On Walpurgis Night, 1966 (April 31), LaVey shaved his head and announced the formation of the Church of Satan.

LaVey has always shown a deft sense of publicity; he achieved wide news coverage when he invited the press to see a marriage performed on an 'altar' which consisted of a naked

girl. Every room in his house in San Francisco had black or
dark red walls, and suitably satanic decorations, such as
skulls or his own sinister paintings.

In 1969 LaVey published his own programme for
moral — or immoral — reform, called *The Satanic Bible*.
This is not, as might be expected, a litany of blasphemy and
abominations, but the kind of book that might have been
produced by a collaboration between Nietzche, Swinburne
and Aleister Crowley. It argues that the devil is a gentleman,
as G.K. Chesterton remarked in a poem (he added 'and does
not keep his word'), and that he is not as black as he is
painted. It goes on to glorify strength and sneer at weakness,
and to insist that man has allowed himself to be bullied by
moralists into denying his healthy impulses. "The Satanist
feels: 'Why not really be honest and if you are going to create
a god in your own image, why not create that god as
yourself?' Every man is a god if he chooses to recognise
himself as one." LaVey, like Crowley, seems to be expressing irritation with the Godly rather than with God, and his
own form of 'Do what you will' seems to stop well short of
De Sade's suggestion that a truly liberated man would enjoy
disembowelling pregnant women or raping children. LaVey
told one interviewer, Hans Holzer, that the Satanist's Devil is
the Devil that is in every man, that part of his nature that
longs for the full satisfaction of wordly pleasures. 'It had
become clear to me', says Holzer, 'that LaVey's Satanism was
not exactly what the term meant in the Middle Ages when it
was a truly depraved cult'. In fact, LaVey's Satanism is close
to that expressed by William Blake in *The Marriage of Heaven
and Hell* ('Energy is eternal delight'), and would have
appealed deeply to that good-natured old hedonist, Anatole
France.

Holzer goes on to describe a 'black mass' performed in
LaVey's sitting room, with a naked girl, her legs apart,
spread comfortably on the altar, while LaVey intoned 'In
nomine dei Satanas. Lucifer excelsi..', and a man in a black
hood sprinkled the congregation with a mixture of urine and
semen, using an instrument shaped like a phallus. The
congregation repeated invocations to Samiel and Moloch,
then a queue of suppliants asked for things they wanted
most — such as a better job, more attention from a girlfriend
and — in one case — the death of an enemy. ('The high
priest nodded gravely, and the request for the man's death
was made, cheerfully supported by the congregation.')

LaVey's Satanic cult underlines the basic problem about
Satanism or Devil worship: that it is, of necessity, enfeebled
by an internal contradiction. Plato stated the view that most
thoughtful human beings would accept, that there is no such
thing as evil *per se*. For all living creatures, 'good means that
which brings satisfaction; for a person to 'do evil' would
mean to pursue the unsatisfying, which seems contradictory.
Men seek their own version of 'the good', and if they happen

to be stupid or corrupt or merely confused, then their satisfactions may well involve inconvenience to other people — and usually to themselves. In short, evil is another name for stupidity.

According to Bernard Shaw, there are two types of moral reformers: those who tell people that something they have always regarded as harmless — like whistling on the Sabbath — is wicked; and those who tell people that something they have always regarded as wicked — like adultery — is harmless. The former type — the Calvins and John Knoxes — cause most misery. The latter type — like Blake, Ibsen and Shaw ·himself — cause a great deal of indignation at the time, and occasionally (like the founder of Mormonism) get lynched; but sensible people usually come to recognise the sense in what they are saying. LaVey, on the whole, belongs with this latter type of moral reformer, and is not therefore a true Satanist (like the Yezidi sect, who genuinely worship the Devil). Even De Sade, who made determined efforts to sound wicked, is widely respected by French intellectuals for his moral courage and honesty — hardly 'evil' qualities.

Magic is a slightly different matter. LaVey told the journalist David St Clair that his attempts at magic enabled him to conjure up parking places in front of theatres, make business deals come his way, and even cause two people to marry when they disliked one another. This has nothing to do with Satan, but with the hidden forces of the human will. (People who practise the Silva method of mind control claim that it can produce similar results — I know an American college professor who swears by it as a method of finding parking spaces.) This was the kind of magic that Crowley himself practised. But it can also be practised quite unconsciously, without any of the usual magical disciplines or rituals. The novelist John Cowper Powys remarks in his autobiography that he soon discovered that awful harm befell people against whom he felt resentment, so that he ended in a state of 'neurotic benevolence', terrified of losing his temper.

At the time of her death, Jayne Mansfield was being groomed by the studio as a successor to Marilyn Monroe, and her lawyer, Sam Brody, had the utmost objection to her involvement in LaVey's Satanic cult, which might cause embarrassment to the publicity department. When he threatened to start a newspaper campaign, LaVey retaliated by pronouncing a solemn ritual curse. He told Brody that he would be dead within a year, and warned Jane Mansfield not to share Brody's car. After her death he commented laconically: 'She was the, victim of her own frivolity'. LaVey's Satanic image was reinforced when he played the Devil in Polanski's film of *Rosemary's Baby;* but his *Satanic Bible,* like his comment on Jayne Mansfield's death, suggests a moral reformer with distinctly puritanical leanings.

149

CHAPTER 32

Brazilian Magic and Witchcraft

An American journalist, David St Clair, has described his first impressions of Rio de Janeiro in 1959. Strolling along with some Brazilian friends, he came upon some burning candles on the pavement, and a small clay statue of the devil. When he reached out to touch the statue a friend grabbed his arm, saying it was 'despacho' — an offering to a spirit. 'But surely you don't believe that?' asked St Clair, 'You're all college graduates.' 'Of course we don't believe in it — but don't touch it all the same.' St Clair soon discovered that even a starving man would not touch the offerings of food placed for the 'spirits' — in the middle of busy streets or on beaches — and he has seen dogs approach the roasted chicken or steak, sniff it, and go away.

In a chapter called 'The Psi Underworld' in *The Indefinite Boundary*, Guy Playfair tells a story of a psychology graduate named Marcia who picked up a small plaster statue of the sea god Yemanja on the beach at Sao Paolo and, against the advice of a friend, took it home. A run of appalling bad luck began as soon as she had placed it on her mantelshelf: first, food poisoning, then tuberculosis, then burns from an exploding pressure cooker, then an exploding oven. She began to experience suicidal urges, having to struggle to prevent herself flinging herself in front of cars or out of a window. Then the bedroom seemed to be full of 'presences' that touched her body under bedsheets; one night, she felt a

Right A Brazilian 'witch doctor' contacting spirit forces.

150

body lying on top of her, and an erect penis penetrated her. It happened again on successive nights. Finally, she decided to visit the local *Umbanda* centre, *Umbanda* being Brazil's own form of voodoo. She took along the statue. The director of the centre told her that her sufferings were 'revenge' for her unlawful removal of the statue, and advised her to take it back to the place where she had found it. When she did this, her life quickly returned to normal.

It was only after the *Umbanda* director warned her about the statue that she noticed something odd: the paint was worn off the face and arms of the statue; patches remained in exactly the same places she had suffered burns; even the 'spot' on her lung corresponded to a remaining patch of paint.

One of the most widespread religions in Brazil is Spiritualism, or (as they prefer to call it) Spiritism; and the Brazilian form is based specifically on the writing of 'the father of Spiritism', Allan Kardec. Kardec's real name was Hypolyte Leon Denizard Rivail, and he became successful in his early twenties when he opened a private school. In 1850, when the excitement about the Fox sisters reached the Continent, Kardec was a highly respected educator in his mid-forties; he became fascinated by 'spirit communications', particularly automatic writing. When two daughters of a friend showed unusual ability in this direction, he persuaded them to devote two evenings a week to 'sitting' with him. It struck him that the resulting body of information constituted a clear and coherent doctrine, based on reincarnation; so he set it all down in a work called *The Spirits' Book;* achieved considerable influence in France for two decades or so after its publication (in 1857) — although Kardec's dislike of trance mediums (whom he regarded as unreliable) retarded the growth of organised psychical research in France. But it gradually became half-forgotten. His work took some decades to reach Brazil; but it seems to have caused far more excitement there than in Europe, and soon became the basis of the Brazilian version of Spiritualism. *Candomble* and *Umbanda* may also be regarded as forms of 'spiritism', but with more in common with voodoo. In fact, a Brazilian may find nothing contradictory in regarding himself as a good Catholic, a Spiritist, and a believer in *Umbanda.*

A representative story of *Umbanda* in action can be found in David St Clair's *Drum and Candle.* He had taken on a pretty Brazilian girl — whom he calls Edna — as a maid - housekeeper, and found her in every way satisfactory; their relationship remained strictly one of employer and employee. She joined a dance group, went on television, and became something of a star; St Clair advised her to 'better herself' instead of remaining in his rather unstable household.

Then things began to go wrong — everything. A book failed to sell, a legacy failed to materialise, a girl spurned him, and his health began to deteriorate. A Brazilian woman told

him that someone had put the evil-eye on him and that 'Your paths have been closed'. And a Spiritist friend who came to stay told him that it was Edna who was responsible. He had learned this at a spiritist session. Edna was determined not to be abandoned by St Clair when he went on a projected trip — she was hoping he would marry her, and had been attending *Quimbanda* — black magic — sessions to that end.

With some difficulty, St Clair induced Edna to take him to an *Umbanda* session — she insisted she knew nothing about such things. In a closed room, there was chanting and the sound of drums. A negro woman came in and danced — the 'witch doctor'; some people began to jerk and moan as they became 'possessed' by spirits. Finally, a 'possessed' medium told him that the person who had 'closed his paths' was the one who had brought him there that night. Edna walked out, whereupon the 'witch doctor' (who insisted she was really a man) sang and chanted to the drums to get rid of the curse.

After that, everything began to go right again; the legacy came, the book sold, the girl who had rejected him asked to come back. But Edna became very ill. She had a growth in her stomach which had to be removed — St Clair paid the bill. An *Umbanda* priest told her that she would remain sick as long as she remained with St Clair — the curse she had put on him had returned two-fold. So Edna walked out.

From St Clair's *Drum and Candle* and Playfair's *The Flying Cow*, it is clear that witchcraft, in the widest and most ancient sense of that word, still flourishes in Brazil.

Playfair remains convinced that Brazilian witchcraft 'works' because the witch-doctors are able to persuade certain 'discarnate entities' to perform services for them. 'Any Brazilian is well aware that the country is full of backyard *terreiros* of *quimbanda* (black magic centres) where people use spirit forces for evil purposes.' After a *candomblé* exorcist had successfully driven out a poltergeist that had practically wrecked a household, he explained that 'an *exu morcego* was a type of pagan spirit dwelling in the shadows, probably that of a former criminal who had nothing better to do than bother people'. Playfair adds: 'Probing into the background of the case, researchers found that as so often where there is a poltergeist, there is, or was, somebody with a grudge..' Another exorcist remarked: 'You can use a knife to cut bread or to cut a man's throat, and so it is with the hidden powers of man.. To produce a successful poltergeist, all you need is a group of bad spirits prepared to do your work for you, for a suitable reward, and a susceptible victim who is insufficiently developed spiritually to be able to resist. Black magic is really a serious social problem in Brazil...'

It is unnecessary to add that if Playfair is correct, it throws a completely new light on the history of European witchcraft.

CHAPTER 33

Afterword

I am personally acquainted with four witches, three practising 'magicians', and with three 'psychics' who would certainly have been burnt as witches four hundred years ago. All of them appear to be perfectly normal human beings, and there is certainly nothing frightening or formidable about any of them.

How does one become a witch? The story of my friend Lois Bourne is probably typical. When she was five, her eldest brother fell to his death from the top of a building, and he later came to her in the garden with his arms outstretched. When she became a nurse, she found she always knew in advance when patients would die, and often saw them after death — in one case she thought the patient had got out of bed until she checked and found that she had died. She felt 'drawn' to reading books on parapsychology, and it gradually became clear to her that she could 'make things happen' if she wanted them enough. She then found it would work for other people; one friend consulted her about her boss, whom she found attractive, but seemed unaware of her existence. Lois got to work with a photograph of the man and two of his hairs — that was all she needed. He quickly invited his secretary to dinner, they spent the night together, and she subsequently married him.

Although she considers herself a white witch — that is, she has never used her powers to do harm — she has to keep a watch on her emotions. In her autobiography *Witch Among Us*, she tells of an occasion when she was trying out a new car, and had stalled it at a traffic light; a man behind her honked loudly and finally shot past her cursing. In a rage she yelled 'Pig, I hope your radiator runs dry.' Three miles further on, she saw the car parked by the roadside, the puzzled driver looking at the radiator, from which steam was pouring.

Now this kind of power is what I am inclined to call a 'controlled poltergeist effect'. After styding Uri Geller, I concluded that this explains his powers — not only of metal bending, but of causing objects to appear out of the empty air (apports). I still keep an open mind about whether such effects are caused by a juvenile delinquent who lives in the right brain, or by 'spirits' in a jocular mood. Lois Bourne believes that 'There is a great residual force within the human body, that it possesses an energy far in excess of its everyday requirements, and that this force can be released by concentration and stilling of the mind'. She also remarks 'One of the greatest barriers to mediumship is the intellect, and the most serious problem I had to learn in my early psychic career was the suspension of my intellect. If, during the practice of extra-sensory perception, I allowed logistics to prevail, and permitted myself to rationalise about the impressions I received, and the things I said, I would be hopelsly lost within a conflict. It is necessary that I totally by-pass my concious mind and allow the subconcious mind to (come to) the surface...'

Another witch of my acquaintance, Marion Weinstein, was fascinated by witches as a child, began to research 'the occult' in high school, and plunged into serious reading — Jung, Gardner, Margaret Murray — during an unhappy period as an actress when her career was marking time. But when I asked her how she first suspected she was a witch, she replied that, as a child of ten or eleven she had noticed 'how things seemed to be able to just 'work out' sometimes when I managed a certain attitude towards a problem, a sort of all-encompassing belief which seemed to take on a life of its own and shape my own life thereby'. She says she wondered how she could control this process, and sees this as the origin of her interest in witchcraft.

So it seems that the decision to become a witch usually starts with an observation — that in certain moments you have an odd flash of power or insight. You may simply 'know' something; or you may know that, in some odd way, you can influence the course of events.

In that sense, I am convinced that witchcraft is less the exception than the rule. I would go further and say that in this sense, we are all witches. Then why is witchcraft relatively rare? The answer, I think, is that few of us attempt to develop these abilities, just as few of us ever learn to ski. And the chief reason is that we find it so hard to believe in such powers. We are inclined to take a naturally pessimistic view of ourselves and our power to influence events. People like Lois Bourne and Marion Weinstein started out with a tiny spark of inborn conviction that they could, in some odd way, influence events, and they have had the courage — and perhaps the romanticism — to try to get to grips with it to understand it more deeply. They became 'witches' by a simple process of personal evolution, just as I became a writer by struggling to express myself until it began to come easily.

This, for me, is the important aspect of witchcraft, the one that deeply influences me. I recognise, at the same time, that there is another, with which I find it far more difficult to come to terms. The late Tom Lethbridge lived next door to a witch in Devon, and one of the things she taught him was how to 'throw pentagrams' — that is, how to carefully 'draw' a pentagram in the imagination. The witch told him that pentagrams have strong defensive powers. One night, Lethbridge lay in bed idly practising drawing pentagrams around the bed. A couple of days later, the witch called on him, and said that somebody had been 'putting protection' on him. He asked why. Because, she said, she had projected her 'astral body' into his bedroom a few nights before, and found the bed surrounded by triangles of fire...

Lethbridge's wife Mina tried using a technique, suggested by the witch, for keeping away unwelcome visitors; she said that all that was necessary was to 'draw' (in your head) an inverted pentagram on the gate, or in the path of the unwelcome guest. Lethbridge himself claims he saw one such guest stop dead in his tracks, then turn and go away. Mina Lethbridge also claims that the method is effective.

When I asked a friend who practices 'magic' what he thought of the idea, he admitted he had never heard of 'throwing' inverted pentagrams on gateposts, but said that it would undoubtedly exercise a repellant effect.

How? I have no idea — any more than I know why a 'charm' from the Bible should enable Fred Martin to cure warts. The answer may lie in the writings of W.B. Yeats, with his suggestions about the connection between symbols and the unconcious, or in the psychology of Jung. As to myself, I am content to regard the 'symbolic' magic as an unsolved mystery. What continues to fascinate me is the mind itself, and our increasingly clear recognition that, like the earth, it contains immense and violent forces beneath the solid-looking crust. Science is an attempt to harness the forces of nature; magic is an attempt to harness the forces of the mind. The history of witchcraft could yet prove to be one of the most important pages in the story of human evolution.

INDEX